POOR TIME MANAGEMENT HOW BRINGS

ORGANIZATIONAL NEGATIVE BEHAIVOR

JOHN LOK

Contents

Preface

I write the book aim to let any working people learn how to dealt personnel challenges when who need to cooperate with their staffs. I shall use different working environments to suppose what the personnel challenges you will face and I also suggest that you ought adopt what personnel solvable methods and positive attitudes to solve these personnel challenges are the best. I shall indicate different organizations' staffs cooperation challenges and I also suggest my best personnel solvable methods to dealt these challenges, for example, movie making team, baseball team, nuclear factory, business office, university, interior decorating partnership , bank, restaurant etc. different organizations.

This book is suitable to be read by managers, CEO, administration clerk, organizational psychology etc. professional. I believe that you can learn how to dealt personnel psychological challenges in your working environments more easily. Finally, as i am one business psychology, i hope that you can learn how to apply psychology knowledge, e.g. expectancy theory, ERG theory, Maslow's hierarchy, path goal leadership theory , Attribute theory ,integration framework ,concept of motivation, goal setting theory ,organizational cultures and subcultures etc. psychology theories to help manager to predict your staffs behavior to know how who will change whose personnel behavior to solve your management challenges in different working environment more easily. I shall apply psychological theory to explain how manager can predict every employee behavior, what reasons cause who chooses to do the decision or behavior in any organization in order to make solvable methods to avoid argument with employees more easily in organization.

Prologue

Table of contents

CHAPTER I

Marketing consultant organization

Describe people related problems or issues, one marketing consultant firm, Ann Wood faced personnel problem during the day. Ann Wood, marketing director faced problem of two senior marketing analysts would leave her marketing research department as well as after these two senior market analysts left her department, it would cause the one urgent and important market analysis was delayed and it was more difficult to finish before the due date. Ann Wood, her marketing research manager, Joe would lack these two senior market analysts continue to assist whose marketing department to help to finish this one important market analysis during the date. The result of the one important market analysis was delayed to finish after the due date. Ann Wood would face her employer felt who could not achieve excellent performance to promote to do this marketing director position to manage her marketing research department to operate successfully. Even, after these two senior marketing analysists decided to leave Ann, marketing director her marketing department during the day. This issue would influence the overall many teams of other marketing analysts and senior marketing analysts who lost more confidence to serve Ann Wood's marketing department to cause it would have many marketing analysts and senior marketing analysts would plan to leave her department after her first working day. However, the major factor caused these two senior marketing analysts decided to leave her department during the day, it is possible that because their office computers were broken down, so they could not use internet to send this important marketing analysis project to let their manager and Ann, marketing director to read by email during the day or they felt their salaries level were below than marketing salary level, so they had planned to leave during Ann wood her first work day . During the day, the reasons of these two senior marketing analysts who planned leaving include that they felt who were very talented in whose job and had won several key projects as proof, so who ought earn higher salary, During the day, after their leaving, some other marketing analysts also planned to leave because who felt these two senior marketing analysts leaving, then they would rise workloads rapidly and they felt the marketing salaries level were higher than their current salaries unfairly. Hence, Ann Wood would face some marketing analysts and senior marketing analysts would leave her department during the day.

Suggestion of solvable methods:

Did she handle these effectively?

I think she did not handle effectively in these people related matters. An effective senior manager needs to spend much time talking with insiders and outsiders about vision, strategy, and other major issues to the direction of the organization. A senior leader needs to make the strategic decision for the firm. Skills in conceptualizing, communicating and understanding the perspectives of others are critical for these discussion. A senior manager also needs spend time helping middle managers to define and redefine their roles and to manage conflict because middle managers are often central to the organization's communication networks. Skills in listening, conflict management, negotiating and motivating are important for these activities. Ann Wood ought attempt to use these methods to handle her staffs personal problems effectively.

Engagement is as the extent to which staffs enjoy and believe in what who do and feel valued for doing it. So, if they feel enjoyment, her staffs tend to receive more pleasure and satisfaction from what who do if who are in jobs or roles that match both their interests and skills. For example, some people like jobs that require travel enjoyment, when some prefer not to travel. Others like a high risk/high reward bonus plan where others prefer a more stable and predictable salary. Some individuals like work in a team environment, others like work more independently. So, Ann Wood (head of marketing) can make questionnaires to enquire every project team members what non financial and financial rewards are who want to get from this employer in order to raise their efficiency to work and reduce the leaving staff numbers in every project team.

In belief, if her staffs felt who were making meaningful contributions to their jobs, their current employer and society. Then, who should tend to be more engaged to the connection between what every project team does every day and the goals and mission of Ann Wood's company can be engaged successfully. Other people related problem is Ann's staffs lack enough marketing research skill and working experience. For example, Ann's one of staff Joe Jackson, the current manager of the market research group, who complained to Ann about the company's intranet had been down about half of the night and this technical problem had prevented timely access to data from a central server, resulting in a delay in the completion of an important market analysis on her first work day. He could not attempt to find any department staffs to help him to solve this problem. He did not know that whose some marketing research projects should delay if who waited Ann arrived office and then enquired her how to solve. Moreover, every marketing team members who ought lack enough marketing research working skills because who have no anyone could have confidence to finish every important and urgent marketing research projects before due date. Otherwise, if they had specialised marketing research skill, they ought spend little time to finish these urgent and important projects. So, the computer technical problem would not influence their projects to be finish. Thus Ann would face that many staffs will leave her department and the important and urgent marketing research projects will be delayed to finish after the due date.

What do I believe she should have done?

On the one hand, Ann only believed Joe, the current manager of the market research group whose suggestions to increase the market analysts salary if she want to increase their speed to finish every marketing research analysis and reducing the market analysts turnover numbers. She had not enquire other different marketing research managers idea why they could not finish every marketing research project quickly. What the problems were caused who are encountered to finish every marketing research project slowly.

On the other hand, Ann could not know what the urgent jobs are who ought need to solve. When Joe, the current manager of the market research group told her that the company's intranet has been broken to cause a delay in the completion of an important market analysis. After she had not attempted to find the computer technical staffs to help her to repair intranet during the day and she still to read any email in her office computer during the day.

I think Ann needed to attempt to find computer technical staffs to help her to repair intranet immediately and she ought not spend much time to see email, she ought continue enquire whether intranet had been repaired and the completion of an important market analysis had been sent during the day and she ought not spend much time to discuss to increase salaries matter to market analysts with Joe during the day. Thus, Ann did not know what the duties are needed to handle urgently during the day effectively.

Is Ann Wood a high involvement manager? provide evidence.

I feel that Ann Wood is not a high involvement manager. From the motivational and leadership practices of managers to the internal dynamic of employee-based teams to the values that provide the base for the organization's culture, successful firms develop approaches that unleash the potential of their people (human capital). However, Ann Wood does not understand the actions of every team individual member and every team group in her marketing research department as well as who also does not understand the actions focused on acquiring, developing, and applying the knowledge and skills of every team members as well as who lacks an approach that involved organizing and managing every team's knowledge and skill effectively

to implement her marketing research department's strategy and gains a competitive advantage. Thus, if Ann, head of marketing director could organize and manage every marketing research team effectively, the knowledge and skills of every marketing research team member in the marketing research department can drive sustainable competitive advantages and long term financial success. For example, Ann's one of staff Joe Jackson, the current manager of the market research group, who complained to Ann about the company's intranet had been down about half of the night and this technical problem had prevented timely access to data from a central server, resulting in a delay in the completion of an important market analysis on her first work day. He could not attempt to find any department staffs to help him to solve this problem. He did not know that whose some marketing research projects should delay if who waited Ann arrived office and then enquired her how to solve. Moreover, every marketing team members who ought lack enough marketing research working skills because who have no anyone could have confidence to finish every important and urgent marketing research projects before due date. Otherwise, if they had specialised marketing research skill, they ought spend little time to finish these urgent and important projects. So, the computer technical problem would not influence their projects to be finish. I think she did not handle effectively in these people related matters.

An effective senior manager needs to spend much time talking with insiders and outsiders about vision, strategy, and other major issues to the direction of the organization. A senior leader needs to make the strategic decision for the firm. Skills in conceptualizing, communicating and understanding the perspectives of others are critical for these discussion. A senior manager also needs spend time helping middle managers to define and redefine their roles and to manage conflict because middle managers are often central to the organization's communication networks. Skills in listening, conflict management, negotiating and motivating are important for these activities. On the one hand, Ann only believed Joe, the current manager of the market research group whose suggestions to increase the market analysts salary if she want to increase their speed to finish every marketing research project and reducing the market analysts turnover numbers. She had not enquire other different marketing research managers idea why they can not finish every marketing research project quickly. What the problems are that who are encountered to cause to finish every marketing research project slowly. On the other hand, Ann could not know what the urgent jobs are who ought need to solve. When Joe, the current manager of the market research group told her that the company's intranet has been broken to cause a delay in the completion of an important market analysis. After she had not attempted to find the computer technical staffs to help her to repair intranet during the day and she still to read any email from her office computer during the overtime of the whole day. It proved that her time management is not effective to deal what the jobs are urgent and what the jobs are not urgent to do during the day.

If no, how well do you think she will perform in her new job as head of marketing?

I think Ann needed to attempt to find computer technical staffs to help her to repair intranet immediately and she ought not spend much time to see email, she ought continue enquire whether intranet had been repaired and the completion of an important market analysis had been sent during the day and she ought not spend much time to discuss to increase salaries matter to market analysts with Joe during the day. Thus, Ann did not know what the duties are needed to handle urgently during the day effectively. The most important, Ann needs to know what kind of job duties who needs to do as she is director of marketing clearly. This marketing research department is an internal department , every project team leader needs to manage and arrange every team member to finish every marketing research project efficiently and effectively. Hence, Ann's main duty ought to assist her every marketing research team to finish every marketing analysis before the due date to avoid to extend time to

finish every important marketing analysis in this marketing department. Ann needs to know individual factors, e.g. learning ability, personality, values, motivation and stress and interpersonal factors, e.g. leadership, communication, decision making skill, intra and inter group
dynamic communications will influence her performance in her new job as director of marketing successfully.

I think Ann Wood ought to perform as these methods in her new job as head of marketing. However, She could attempt to produce a fair job description, it's an internal part of job evaluation process, grading and salary description, training is focused on elements of a job and how employees can perform better in their job. Aim to produce a reasonable salary to compare market salary level in every specific positions. Job analysis is establishing and defining every position correctly is from the starting point. Enquiring employees to complete questionnaires, observing and interviewing people. It aims to enlarge job enrichment, it extends the work of existing employees to cover more responsibility and decision making. Motivation is the act of getting someone to act on a situation in a workplace. Maslow's hierarchy of needs includes these level:

The first level is physiological needs are basic
needs to be met in order to survive, including food, water, clothing, sleep and shelter.

The next level is security, staffs' surroundings are not threatening to them or family. If the environment seems to be safe, then it means stability in the workplace. Security could also include financial security. This could be achieved by creating a retirement package, securing job position and insurance.

The third level is affiliation which is the need to feel a since of belonging or to be loved. In the workplace, this means to feel as though they are a part of the group and included in the work. The fourth level is explained as esteem. This is the view that one has of themselves, the person must have a high image of them self and encompass self respect. Feelings of self worth and the need for respect from others. The last and final stages of the hierarchy of needs is self actualization . This level is defined as someone being all they can be and they have met each of the previous stages. The person's talents are being completely utilized. The growth needs or the highest level of needs are the only real motivators of employees. Employees feel dissatisfied, so who unmotivated. For an employee to be true motivated, the employee's job has to be fully enriched where the employee has the opportunity for achievement and recognition, stimulation, responsibility and advancement.

Ann Wood can apply Maslow's hierarchy of needs motivation theory to satisfy whose staffs personal needs. She needs to make her staffs to understand that Ann (their head of marketing) feels they are important to this company by financial and non financial types of motivation in workplace compensation to them. Ann Wood (head of marketing) can attempt to implement these types of motivation into her specific new workplace. Her workplaces are suffering with employees who are unmotivated and overall work performance is failing. Currently her employees do not have organizational commitment, then there is no incentive to excel at their own personal goals and organizational goals. If these employees can discuss techniques are implemented in the specific work sites and she needs to make employees have not feel as though who have reached in the end of their career job satisfaction. Thus, her employees feel dissatisfactory to their jobs and they feel financial and non financial rewards are not fair to compare other employers in this market salary level to cause they intend to quit their current employer. She can use quantitative performance measurement to measure her employee work performance, such as absenteeism, project production turnover, extra hours worked as well as qualitative measurement, such as
supervisor/manager ratings on appropriate performance . She can predict her staffs who feel dissatisfactory to their jobs from these information in order to enquire their needs. Often, the measurement will be used in part depend on what work outcomes are regarded as beneficial by her organization. For example, she can use rating form to evaluate every project team members of every one whose job performance from their marketing manager after every project team has finished its project. In conclusion, I give these suggestions to change her performance to deal her new job as head of marketing. For example: Removing some job controls, increasing worker accountability for them own work, giving workers free choice which projects who have interest to finish early, giving greater job freedom or additional authority to every project team members, making periodic reports directly to every project teams (not through every project team leader), introducing new and more difficult projects to give to the more potential project team members and assigning specialized projects to more potential project team members to attempt to finish, so who can become

experts.

Assume Ann Wood wants her managers and associate to be the foundation for her department's competitive advantages. Use framework summarized to assess the degree to which Ann's people are a source of competitive advantage at the point of time. Competitive advantage means four key attributes: values, rarity, a lack of substitutes, difficult to imitate. Human resources are seen to be valuable, the cost of replacing employees who leave organization is high, who are experienced and are seen by clients as important. It results when an organization can perform some aspect of its work better than competitors or when it can perform the work in a way that competitors can't duplicate. The resource based view of organization theory refers the nature of human resource can be regarded as uniquely valuable to organization because who are a collection of asset (skills, competencies and experience) and are much more difficult to replicate, unlike other conventional asset, such as land or capital. Rarity is value or be a labour group which is short supply. Organizations have as stable supply of skills in short supply will have a competitive advantage. It is difficult to imitate skilled work of employees, change of services can be available. In instant, self service in restaurant but the market for high quality service by skilled employees are constant growth (Stredwick . J, 2005).

Human capital rareness means the extent to which the skills and talents of an organization's people are unique in the industry as well as human capital imitability means the extent to which the skills and talents of an organization's people can be copied by other organizations. Thus, Ann needs to employ staffs who are valuable, rare and difficult to imitate. If Ann want to lead her marketing research department efficiently. She needs to ensure every team leader has leadership ability and their marketing research skills and talents are unique in this marketing research industry as well as every team member marketing research skills and talents can not be copied by other competitors.

Thus, aims to assess the degree to which Ann's people are a source of competitive advantage at the point of time, who can follow these steps: Firstly, Ann Wood, head of marketing, who can attempt arrange training program is both quantitatively and qualitatively. Such training provides the base for effective of discretion by every marketing research team member. Reward systems that value in individual and team every project productivity help to encourage the type of behaviour that is desired. Giving responsibility and accountability complement the system. It aims to make every marketing research team member who can believe project should be fulfilling before due date, workplace should be fearless and energized, work and family life should be balanced and every project team leader should serve followers, every project team members should be treated like customers and who should not be afraid to make mistakes. This training program aims to achieve further lower turnover, higher satisfaction and stronger motivation among every project team members.

I feel the degree to which Ann's people are a source of competitive advantage at the point of time is not high. The reasons include as below: For example, Ann's one of staff Joe Jackson, the current manager of the market research group, who complained to Ann about the company's intranet had been down about half of the night and this technical problem had prevented timely access to data from a central server, resulting in a delay in the completion of an important market analysis on her first work day. He could not attempt to find any department staffs to help him to solve this problem. He did not know that whose some marketing research projects should delay if who waited Ann arrived office and then enquired her how to solve. Moreover, every marketing team members who ought lack enough marketing research working skills because who have no anyone could have confidence to finish every important and urgent marketing research projects before due date. Otherwise, if they had specialised marketing research skill, they ought spend little time to finish these urgent and important projects. So, the computer technical problem would not influence their projects to be finish. Hence, I think Ann needs to give them training to raise their marketing research skill if she still hope they can have high degree of competitive abilities to finish every further marketing research projects before due date.

Reference

Stredwick. J, (2005). An Introduction to human resource management. Elsevier Ltd, UK.

CHAPTER II

Baseball team organization

What happened with the A team ?

One basketball A-team workload was sufficiently heavy to make task interdependence necessary and their performance outcomes (i.e. grades) were important to individual's academic standing (i.e. they were probation consequences for low team grades) and job prospects (for both recruitment and tuition reimbursement). Thus, when there were student teams, the work were a reasonable simulation of business teams with both task related work as well as social relationship and reputation consequences if the groups failed.

The fact that the A-team was newly forming and began their work with the same baseline resources was also important to this study in terms of differentiating the effectiveness of team conflict management strategies. Although A-team who have different expertise, but they have conflict due to different educational background and working experiences to cause A-team members cooperation will be more difficultly.

Why did the group process break down?

This group process broke down because every member have different educational background and working experiences in their expertise field. They did not discuss who could do this team leader clearly For example, Aran suggested he could attempt to do this A-team leader because he was a management consultant in one large firm and his age was 52 year older than other four members, but the four members who could not agree his suggestion because they also had their expertise educational background and working experience. It should cause diversity conflict between of them. So, this group could not continue to discuss successfully.

What dimensions of diversity were responsible for the conflict?

Diversity is often defined in terms of particular dimensions, most commonly gender, race, and ethnicity, Other important dimensions also exist. These include age, social class, sexual orientation, personality, functional experience (e.g., finance, marketing, accounting), and geographical background. Visible attributable (e.g. race, gender, ethnicity), attributes directly related to job performance (e.g. education and functional experience), and rare attributes are the most likely to be seen as important.

Workplace diversity could be a valuable asset for a organizational growth and development, e.g. age discrimination, not equal employment opportunity. Everyone has an equal chance at employment regardless of race, sex, religion, national original.

suggestion of solvable method:

In this university MBA A-team students team, the dimensions of diversity were responsible for the conflict were as the different groups of these five students should be treated equally that rewards should be based on merit (university project result) and decision maker (team leader) should be blind to the sex or ethnicity of MBA students to arrange their different roles and job duties to carry on doing this business plan project in their university. Hence, workplace diversity management can apply to this university MBA students diversity management. Workplace equal employment opportunity is similar to this university MBA A-team five students equal roles and duties opportunity as well as workplace organization decision maker is similar to this university .MBA A-team students team leader who needs to decide either employees or MBA A-team student team

members to pay attention to characteristics like sex or ethnicity to determine if who affect employment consequences or to arrange university MBA A-team five student members every role and duty to finish this business plan project. In workplace, every employer needs special actions , such as hiring the ethnic minority candidate when applicants appear to have equal qualifications, are considered appropriate requirements to remedy the effects of past discrimination and thus attain equal opportunity.

Thus, this university ought feel that it was such one employer, it needed to help A-team to choose one MBA student for A-team leader from whose prior working experiences and qualification. Then, it needed to give reasons to these other four A-team student members to explain why it felt this MBA student was the best right applicant for their A-team leader. University professor Bowell group advisor might give probation period to this student leader if this A-team four members complaint this team leader who could not serve in the executive function to assign and oversee everyone's work and gave the presentation at end of project. Then , professor Bowell this team advisor might suggest them to select another new leader, so this A-team would not be disbanded easily. As this university selects the right applicant for every position. It needs committee to assist its selection processing. If the dean determines that the committee lacks diversity , it can be reconstituted by including persons from other departments or even other universities. The search committee chair must review information from candidates to ensure that minority and female and male applicants are in the pool. The dean's office reviews applications of diverse candidates of none of them appears among the search committee's choices of candidates to be interviewed, the committee must provide an explanation. Finally, the university team advisor ought be similar to an employer who needs to choose who are the top student candidates (employees) to make A-team (job offer) from their educational background, working experiences. It aims to reduce dimensions of diversity were responsible for the conflict.

Describe which barriers to effectively managing diversity were present in this situation?

Diversity can be defined as a characteristic of a group of people where differences exist on one or more relevant dimensions such as gender. First, faults can be present in situations characterized by diversity. Faults occur when two or more dimensions of diversity are correlated. For example, if all /most of the young people on a cross-functional task force represent marketing when all/most of the older individuals represent product engineering, then a fault is said exist. Faults merge multiple identifies (e.g. young and marketing focused) to produce barriers to effective collaborations within a group. Research on this phenomenon is relatively new, but has produced findings suggestion poor group outcomes. It can be applied to this A-team university team members conflict what barriers are to effectively managing diversity were present in this situation.

The barriers to effectively managing diversity were present in this situation , it is possible that this A-team group members who have different educational and working backgrounds to cause barriers to effectively managing diversity in this situation. For example, Rebecca is a young marketing manager for a large and high end Italian fashion company. She hopes this university MBA course can help her to be promoted to an executive position as well as Aran is 52 year old founder and CEO of an management consultant firm. He hopes this university MBA course can help him to retire from his consulting firm earlier and become an in house information system consultant to a large multinational firm. When she knew Aran promoted him to be this A-team leader because he had the most experience and he should serve in the executive function. Thus, he would assign and oversee every member's work and he would also give the presentation at the end of this project. Although, Aran have more confident to give reasons why he is the best person choice to be this team leader to manage every member and he also give useful suggestion that Cameron, an internet entrepreneur who heads his own small but successful company who will be in charge of analysing the financial feasibility of their project, developing the marketing plan, and evaluating the technical operations and the other members need to assist him. However, Aran is one managing consultant and Rebecca is one young marketing manager. Aran's educational and working experience is related to information system, but Rebecca educational and working experience is related to marketing field. Thus they have different expertise and skill. Rebecca feels that she has marketing field experience and she is younger than Aran. So, she have more ability than Aran to attempt to do a team leader to manage this A-team members how to produce marketing plan and report and presentation effectively. In conclusion, because these five students have different educational and working experience in their expertise field, so they feel themselves has ability to attempt to be team leader or attempt to do their job duties who prefer to choose by themselves. It will cause difficulty to any one team leader to manage diversity in this A-team members effectively and successfully.

CHAPTER III

Interior decorating partnership organization

What did Teresa learn?

One interior decorating partnership, Teresa learned her interior decorating partnership have these barriers to cause failure. They include as limited vision/ failure to inspire, one partner manipulates or dominates or partners complete for the lead, lacking of clear purpose to understand purpose, lacking of understanding roles/ responsibilities, lacking of support from another partner's decision making power, differences of philosophies and manners of working, lacking of commitment, unwilling participants, unacceptable balance of power and control, key interests and/or people missing from the partnership, failure to communicate and learn, lacking of evaluation or monitoring systems, financial and time commitments outweigh potential benefits and too little time for effective consultation. Due to result of her interior decorating partnership business is not successful and more conflict, so Teresa ought learn her interior decorating partnership business have these weaknesses, such as that her organizational structure is inefficient, lacking rules of conduct, e.g. good communication between their two partners and their staffs, lacking regular attendance of meeting, continuity of personnel regular transfer of information among the partners, no enough knowledge and ideas are shared within them, lacking adequate financial and human resources are available for implementation, lacking good practice in financial controls, accounting procedures, lacking a learning culture is fostered ,e.g. one of two partners are able to learn from one another by allowing new ideas to come forward in an open exchange of experiences, resources, responsibilities and tasks may differ, but lacking added value of their two partners of each is recognised. Thus, Teresa's interior decorating partnership business is likely to be ineffective because these two partners don't share the same values and interests to cause goals difficult, there is no sharing of risk, responsibility, accountability or benefits between of them, the inequalities in partners' resources and expertise determine their relative influence in their decision making, one person or partner has all the power and/or drives the process. It causes the another partner feels unfair, there is a hidden motivation which isn't declared to them, these two partners don't have the training to identify issues or resolve internal conflicts these two partners are not chosen carefully particularly of it is difficult to de partner. Hence, Teresa had learned why another partner changes attitude to perform poor behaviour to expect to achieve to dissolve this interior decorating partnership business successfully because who had different ideas or vision to cause their business operations could not achieve efficiently daily in the beginning.

suggestion of solvable method:

Quitting, What can Teresa do to resolve the problem? What learning and perception factors should she consider as she analyse the situation?

The learning perception factors include that Teresa should consider as she analyses the situation as : She needs to know that the another partner, Vegas within her interior decorating partnership business should know precisely why who are there, what who bring to the alliance, what to expect from others and what is to be achieved together or what is expected of them, she needs to know clarification as to the roles and functions of her further another new partner, so what roles and functions are important to her new partnership. In relation of cooperation factor, she needs to know that she and another new partner can take on various functions , knowledge carriers, information brokers, financiers and policy makers and various roles, visionaries, strategists, salesmen and coaches etc. However , facilitators, mediators and not least, managers are also essential to the functioning of her new interior decorating partnership business. Every individual partner usually has more than one role and function, for example, a partner can act as a knowledge carrier, financier and visionary at the same time. In addition, the roles and functions are important to the overall success of the partnership. If not instance a partnership lacks salesman, it will not be able to communicate its output in the best way. Similarly, partnerships without moderators will almost certainly run into difficulties co-ordinating and balancing the partners' inputs. It is important that roles and functions are clarifies in advance, each partnership should discuss, precisely define and jointly decide on the roles that each partner has the functions that are necessary for their partnership. Hence, Teresa needs to considerate these learning and perception factors in order to co-operate partnership business more successfully which include ensuring partners who have clear vision and purpose, ensuring who can dominate or who can complete for the leadership to their partnership business, ensuring each partner who can understand whose roles and responsibilities clearly, who have decision power and authority to operate their business before Teresa decides to do new partnership business again.

If you were an outside consultant to the firm could you recommend solutions that might not occur to Teresa or Vegas?

What would they are?

These two partners shall occur conflict and one partner shall sue another partner as their assets and liabilities are separated because one partner plan to dissolve this interior decorating partnership business. In any business situation, there are often a number of different ideas about the way to proceed. Only one way can be chosen. However, discussing different ideas will lead to the best choice. During discussion some problems may arise: Is it good to defend an idea which is apparently not the best choice?

There may be conflict between different levels in an organization's hierarchy or between different departments (some ideas are from which may not be welcome). Partnership purpose is a shared common vision and purpose that builds trust and openness and recognizes the value and contribution of all members also needs to exist. Additionally, shared and decision making processes, extending the scope of influence over and involvement with other services and activities will prove essential to Teresa and Vegas partners' interior decorating business partnership business. Culture and values sharing, understanding and an acceptance of differences (e.g. values, ways of working) are all key components of a successful partnership. Learning and development is a healthy partnership promotes an atmosphere of learning. This may involve monitoring and evaluation aimed at improving members' performance. Investing in partner skills, knowledge and competence needs to be highly valued within the partnership. If I was an outside consultant to the firm I should recommend these solutions of conflict management to their

team that might not occur to cause dissatisfaction and underperformance to Teresa or Vegas. The first step in evaluating a potential partnership is to recognize and agree upon the needs as: identifying principal desired partnership achievements, identifying the factors with successful partnership development, identifying any principal barriers to the partnership, acknowledge and recognize the extent of dependency upon individuals to achieve goals, focus on partnership added value. For example, how can Teresa and Vegas partners achieve more or better results through collaboration? The emphasizing clarity of leadership, whoever leads the development of the partnership needs to be recognized and empowered by whose own partnership business and trusted by the partners. Providing clarity in understanding, framework, culture, values and the approach of partner organizations will need subject of explicit discussion. Partners need to be clear about and understand roles and responsibilities, defining who does what regarding delivery of activities, recognizing and allowing the differences in culture/practise that exist among partners, recognizing and accepting that another partner has a diversity of skills and innovative abilities, e.g. only address significant differences and the lack of coordination of different planning and decision making processes within their implementation of partnership strategies/ activities.

Ensuring their partnership of interior decorating business is built on a shared and common vision and mutually agreeable service principles, ensuring that these two partners understand and agree on the purpose and outcome of this interior decorating partnership business, everyone must have a shared vision regarding why this interior decorating partnership was needed to be developed and what it hopes to achieve to build commit, developing a shared decision making process in which partners have equal power. Decisions should not be the result of consensus based on the lowest common denominator, defining clear partnership aims and objectives as outcomes for users, ensuring that their partnership aims and objectives are realistic, publicizing agreed upon and understanding common aims and priorities, acknowledging the existence of separate connection to jointly agreed aims and objectives. Ensuring a level of ownership and management commitment from the senior level in this partner organization, e.g. directors, executive officers, managers staffs to supervise these two partners behaviour are fair conduct to do every decisions and activities, developing clear partnership's working arrangement result in a clear outcome and maintain value for the contribution of these two partners, avoiding domination of particular

members of this interior decorating partnership business. They must emphasize clarity of roles and responsibilities when valuing the separate roles and the different experience and skill levels required, e.g. ensuring awareness in the financial and non monetary resources each partner brings to these interior decorating partnership business , distinguishing between single and joint responsibilities and accountabilities and ensuring that the prime focus is on process and outcomes and is not structure and inputs. Finally, following an agreement by the partners, ensuring that the purpose, role, responsibility of these two partners, main aims, objectives and outcomes for these partnerships are documented within whatever medium this partnership requires, e.g. business plan, terms of reference or institution. These two partners ought to agree at the outset regarding how who are to measure their success and how who are to incorporate the measurements into the best value requirement for continuous improvement. This measurement process must include arrangements for monitoring and reviewing how effectively this partnership business itself is working. For example, changing personal style (personal behaviour). Both partners need to change their style if they want to become effective team players. Arranged a one-on-one meeting with the dominant executive to gather feedback to their staffs and gives opinions to let these two partners to discuss. Aims to find solutions to get results, such as sales went up , they got costs under control, they actually exceeded their target for profitable growth. Establishing human resource department to support these interior decorating partnership business. It's multiple interior decorating products and design services and geographies business expanding in the future if these two partners want to continue to do this business successfully. Aims to expanded internationally

and even have not face new competition from abroad as their interior decorating products and services rapidly commoditize. As their partnership business becomes more complex, so must be human resource department that support them. The design of the HR department must parallel the many dimensions of business. It aims to build strong functional/ interior decorating product/design service expertise when aligning around customer segments, design in flexibility without adding cost. Each part of the business partner model has a distinct mandate and set of measures. The staff members in each part require difficult sets of skills for success. From an organization design perspective, it makes sense to separate then into distinct units, so it allows for focus and the development of deep skills. Thus, HR is as one function and expects to receive service, whether it is the resolution of a payroll issue or support for an organizational change project and it is about out team and it owns the client relationship.

CHAPTER IV

Bank organization

Bank organization, What role did personality play in the situation at the bank ?

Personality is a stable set of characteristics representing the internal properties of an individual. These characteristics, or traits are relatively, are major determinants of behaviour and influence behaviour across a wide variety of situation. The personality played role in the situation at the bank as: Marian, new employee of this bank loan manager, although she had more experienced in bank loan department, but she could not deal how to persuade this bank eight sections of managers to discuss how to solve loan volumes decreasing trouble successfully and meeting was poor performance and these was no result within eight months. Finally, she decided to enquire Vince Stoddard, the bank president to give suggestion
to her how to persuade them to attend any meeting and how to persuade Dave, loan manager to assist her. Hence, she could not perform that she was one experienced person to have ability to solve any staffs personal trouble in this bank loan department within eight months successfully. I think she had an emotional instability trait, the degree to her to handle this issue stressful and she handled high demand situation with difficult. It influenced her job performance poorly and she could not success to work with this bank loan eight sections of managers ,so she could not feel job satisfaction. Her lower levels of emotional instability tended to be negative due to she needed to find bank president to help her to solve this staff meeting trouble easily and she could not attempt to solve staff meeting to discuss how to increase loan volumes by herself within these eight months. Dave, the bank old loan manager and other seven sections of loan managers, whose personalities were non-agreeableness trait. Agreeableness is the degree to which a person is easy going and tolerant, who believes in the honesty of others, willing to help others and not tend to make conflict and is sensitive to the feelings of others. Due these bank eight sections of loan managers who did not like to attend meeting with Marian to discuss how to solve loan volumes decreasing trouble and there were no any solutions and Dave, this bank old loan manager who does not like to assist Marian to solve this trouble. Thus, I think they are non-agreeableness trait to play in the

situation at this bank.

suggestion of solvable method:

Which the big five personality traits most clearly influenced Marian and Dave?

The big five personality dimensions and the job satisfaction to staffs which have close relationship. Individuals have stable traits that significantly influence their affective and behavioural reactions to organizational settings. Generally, employees who are high in openness, conscientiousness to be more satisfied with their job. Job satisfaction means a pleasurable or a positive emotional stable resulting from the appraisal of one's job or job experience. How the big five personality traits influence job satisfaction and to be able to derive recommendations an recruitment, selection and placement of employees. It relies on factors such as co-workers, promotions and salaries as the only factors that may have an impact on job satisfaction. But the individual difference which is the personality of an individual. It can affect job satisfaction. It assumes that when an individual is in a job situation that suits whose personality who is more satisfied. Personality traits can be described in terms of five basic factors, which are extraversion, agreeableness, conscientiousness, neuroticism and openness to experience job satisfaction relationship of personality traits. In terms of applying personality to the personal environment fit conceptualization , it is important to consider that certain jobs and job tasks require different personality traits. A job which involves a great deal of interpersonal relations may require an individual to be agreeable and extraverted in order to perform at a high level. For example, individuals who are extraverted may have a strong ability to deal with job tasks of an interpersonal nature. If individuals are high on a given personality trait, they will have a preference for job characteristics which are in live with this personality trait. If these preferences are matched with the characteristics of the job, a high characteristics will then activate the relevant personality traits and this activation will lead to increased motivation and therefore result in increased job performance and job satisfaction. In contrast a low satisfactory personal environment fit is likely to result in dissatisfaction and ultimately leaving the occupation. For example, in the banking sectors employees hold different positions. These may include tellers, tellers' supervisors, customer service and sales consultants, branch and assistant managers, loan officers and clerks. This model can be forced on how personality affects job satisfaction . Hence, the personal environment fit suggests that these be a match between individual's personality and the positions they occupy.To give a general view or assumption, it can be said that an effective loan officer or bank teller must have an extraverted personality, as extroverts are warm, exhibit positive emotions and are sociable, hence,who perform well in sociable environments. On banking loan consultants may have a low neuroticism personality, as low neurotic individuals are self confidents and tolerant to stress, hence, it helps them to build credibility and trust with clients. Also, one may say that bank loan department managerial positions, as Marian and Dave may require an individual who is high on agreeableness traits , as who are concerned with others' well being. Hence, they create fair environment and overall one can stay in all positions individuals may have a conscientiousness personality , as this provides for aiming for achievement, acting dutifully being. organized and efficient. Therefore, personality affects how individuals gain satisfaction with their work.

The big five personality traits which most clearly influenced Marian and Dave include that: For example, in the case of bank employee loan manager, Marian and Dave who have an extraversion personality will be satisfied as whose job allows who to be friendly and communicate directly with whose clients. Therefore, one can agree that personality has an effect on the way individuals perform whose work. For another example, if a person has a openness personality trait who will look for work which allows for innovation and creative thinking, such as being an artist or working in formation technology. In conclusion, due to bank is a bank offering financial services to clients industry. Hence, employees' personalities and job satisfaction can influence bank productivity and service quality directly as well as the big five personality traits which are neuroticism, agreeableness, openness, conscientiousness and extraversion of every employee personal characteristics are absolutely related to influence how their work behaviour and attitude to serve their bank client.

Which of the cognitive and motivational aspects of personality played at role ?

The personal environment fit theory has been identified as a way of studying the fit between the job characteristics and the abilities and needs of the individual holding the job. Job satisfaction, organizational commitment, career commitment and career satisfaction are significantly stable over time. Thus, it is possible that what causes individuals to feel satisfied or dissatisfied within themselves. The concept of the personal environment fit basically indicates characteristics of people and their environment results in a positive outcome for both individual and organization.This may mean that a good fit may lead to organization effectiveness and high performance at the same time employees will be satisfied with their work which leads to self actualization and lower stress levels.

Working within the bounds of her personality, what should Marian have done when trouble first seemed to the brewing?

Personality is defined as those feelings, thought, desires and tendencies toward behaviour that contribute to a person's individuality. Marian personality should seem to be the kind of person who did not know how to solve any problem independently . She was usually in control of her behaviour , but it was not easy to control her internal emotion. She knew her emotion reaction to report of executive office when she found any unsatisfactory behaviours from her colleagues and she would be free to think about the problem and made a decision about solving it immediately. It could be found these issues from her past behaviours. For example, she had joined bank eight months ago, as a manager in charge of eight loan sections.

In fact, bank loan volumes were still decreasing during Marian had worked in the bank eight months. Although, she had attempt to call a staff meeting with all of the eight loan section managers, she began to explain that loan volumes were reducing to let them to know to help her to solve this issue, but even, then each subsequent meetings were poor and did not improve. Finally, she asked Vince Stoddard bank president to help her to attempt how to solve staff meeting trouble, but he hadn't been very friendly to give suggestion to her to solve. Otherwise, he was waiting for her to take solution. Hence, Marian should have done foolish behaviour to enquire Vince Stoddard president to help her to solve staff meeting trouble, she could not attempt to solve independently. This issue influenced Vince Stoddard president felt that she was not an experienced and good ability loan manager to help whose bank to achieve to increase loan application volumes successfully.

How should she have maintained Dave's job satisfaction and commitment?

Personality refers to the totality an individual's behavioural and emotional characteristic, moods, attitude, options, motivations and style of thinking, perceiving, speaking and acting. Personality influences how others interact with individuals and how they evaluate and reward or punish them . Hence, personality affects how individuals experience work events to feel job satisfaction and commitment from their employer. Job satisfaction defined the extent to which employees like their work. It includes the employees

like their work. It includes the different aspects of the jobs , such as promotion, opportunities or relation to colleagues. Lack of job satisfaction among employees lead to less productivity, low employee retention, high absenteeism and low morale. A lack of job satisfaction resulting in a low level of employee commitment, impact on performance and the achievement of organizational goals. Low job satisfaction may result in low productivity, high absenteeism, labour unrest and industrial action and high labour turnover. There is a relation between personality and job satisfaction among bank employees. Bank organizations in recruiting, selecting and placing of employees in their jobs , who will be a person job fit to avoid dissatisfaction. Job satisfaction influences an organization's well being with regard to job productivity, employee turnover, absenteeism and life satisfaction. Therefore it is crucial to understand how personality traits affects job satisfaction to improve the selection, recruitment and placing processes in organizations. It also helps individuals to choose their field of study with an understand of their personality to avoid dissatisfaction as it impacts negatively on their working lives. These aspects of employees feeling to this bank is very important to cause their service attitude to clients and work efficiency, job satisfaction aspect , such as remuneration, promotion, work and supervision relationship. Hence, Marian ought attempt to let Dave to feel they are the working partnership (loan manager partners) relationship and are not the work and supervision relationship. It can be concluded that in order for Marian's new bank employer to be successful in their operation. She must be equipped with quality personnel and able to provide good services to the clients. In this ever increasingly, competitive, complex and challenging business environment, this bank needs to ensure it retains its current , profitable old loan applicant clients (increase new loan application customers retention) in order to survive support and loyalty from clients are ensured through acceptable client service. Hence, Marian ought have openness and agreeableness attitude to invite this bank loan department Dave manager and other managers to enquire them why who have no time to attend her meeting regularly individually in her room and she also ought attempt to give some suggestions to them how to increase loan application client numbers. Hence, her one to one individual meeting can avoid who indicate having none any time reason to attend regular meeting together again and she can make Dave , this bank manager feel she doesn't need he assists her and she can deal this difficult issue independently to her employer. I recommend that Marian, this bank new loan department manager, who ought attempt to change Dave, this bank old loan department manager's working attitude to make him to have more job satisfaction and commitment. She aims to encourage he can attempt to increase his confidence to lead his loan department team to increase further loan applicant numbers and making him to feel that Dave is a experienced loan manager and only he has ability to assist Marian how to solve loan application volumes decreasing and increasing payment problem.

How should Marian proceed now that the situation has become very difficult?

Generally, banks offer five main categories of services, namely cash accessibility, asset security, money transfers , loans and financial advice . Marian will work in this loans and financial advice department in this bank. Banks need to make asset security to their clients through safes and by securing the safety of money deposits. Money transfers refer to the banking service of moving clients funds from one account to another, including payment services to external parties. A bank needs to provide the service of loans to its clients.lastly, banks provide financial advice, including advice on investments, wills, taxation, leasing, mergers and personal financial planning. Hence, loan lending service is among of one aspect of bank service to its clients.This bank exists problems of loan applicant numbers were reducing and loan department staffs did not like to go to meeting regularly. It was possible that who felt client numbers are decreasing to lend loans from this bank. It was not serious to influence their job performance directly. They could cause ability to be similar to a team cooperation to threaten Marian , new loan manager to force them to go to attend meeting regularly.

Marian needs to consider change management of this bank loan department manager, Dave's personality and team leadership skill. Her changing must be realistic, achievable and measurable. Before, Marian decided to work in this bank loan department manager position first day. Marian needed to ask her these questions:

What did she want to achieve with this change?
Why and how would she know that the change has been achieved?
Who was affected by this change?
How would they react to it?
How much of the bank loan department change could it achieve loan volumes increasing outcome?
What parts of her change did she need help with?

She needed to consider this issues because these aspects related strongly to her management of personality to Dave loan manager as well as whether loan volumes could be increased from her leadership. Psychological contract theory, which helps to explain the complex relationship between an organization and its employees. However, Marian ,the new bank loan manager has responsibility for managing change, the employee doesn't have a responsibility to manage change because Dave's responsibility is no other than to do whose best, which is different for every loan department managers and depends on a wide variety of factors (health, maturity, stability, experience, personality, motivation etc). Her responsibility for managing

her bank loan department change is with management and executives of her bank loan application increasing volumes and organizational department and she must manage her bank loan department change in a way that all loan department managers can cope with it. Hence, she has a responsibility to facilitate and enable her bank loan department and then to help her loan department all eight section managers to understand reasons and aims to ways of responding positively according to every team of loan manager's own situation and capabilities. Increasingly every loan manager's role is to interpret, communicate and enable, not to instruct and impose which nobody really responds to well. Her change includes mindset change and changing people's mindsets or changing attitudes, because it often indicates a tendency towards imposed or enforced change (theory X) and it implies strongly that her new bank employer's loan department believes that its loan department managers and loan consultants and loan clerks etc staffs currently have the wrong mindset. If these staffs were not approaching their tasks or their loan organizational department effectively, then the loan department has the wrong mindset, not the staffs. Changing is such as new structures, policies, targets, re-locations, etc all create bank new systems and working environment, which need to be explained to her loan department staffs as early as possible, so that her loan department staffs' validating and refining the changes themselves can be obtained. Whenever, the bank new loan employee manager, Marian , her loan department imposes new things on her staffs, there will be difficulties. Participation, involvement and open easily, full communication are the important factors.Thus, if Marian hoped to change hew new bank employer eight loan managers, included Dave manager whose every personal attitude successfully, she needed involve and agree support from these staffs within system (system means environment, processes, culture, relationships, behaviours etc), whether personal or loan organizational department) ; she needed to understand where she and her bank loan department was at the moment and she also needed to understand where she wanted to be, when, why and what the measures would be for having got there; her plans development to loan department e.g. job reorganization, task analysis, job transfer due to information technological development or outsourcing etc which needed to toward in an appropriate achievable measurable stages and she needed to communicate, involve, enable and facilitate involvement from her loan department all staffs as early and openly and as fully as is possible. Marian, she is as a leader (manager) in her new employer, bank loan department to anticipate with eight sections of loan managers to discuss loan decreasing volumes issue. She ought not to be an autocratic leader to use strong, directive, laissez faire actions to enforce the rules, regulations and relationships in her work environment. She ought be a path-goal leader , she needs to select the most appropriate style from directive style or supportive style participative style or achievement oriented style to help her loan department managers and consultants, clerks etc different position staffs (followers) to clarify the paths that lead them to work and achieve personal goals.Hence, loan department every staffs are assigned to positions to allocate whose authority and responsibility, depending on qualifications are assessed by examination or training and working experience fairly. It aims to build their confidence to continue to serve their current bank employer.

CHAPTER V

Puma corporation organization

Frances Mead , compensation director for Puma corporation , who paid well to hire Don Coggin to fill position of benefits administrator for her company in corporate personnel department at Puma, headquartered in Salt Lake city, Utah and the job was located in Utah. Hence, Don could always enjoyed the outdoor and he liked to backpack, camp and did some mountain climbing sport entertainment conveniently. Hence, it ensured that this job location could give Dan to enjoy his likely mountain climbing ,camp, backpack sport entertainment conveniently was also an important reason to influence Don to choose this job.In fact, Dan's financial background aided him greatly in his new benefits administrator job, where he was responsible for development and administration of the pension plan, life and health insurance package, employee stock purchase plan and other employee benefit programs within one month. Dan has learned how to do duties. Frances Mead, she was satisfied with her selection for Dan to do this benefits administrator position. Hence, she expected Dan to move up to in the department rank rapidly, but Dan only concern was that who did not seem to have enough time to enjoy his outdoor activities after he had seem promoted to do further duties absolutely. It implied that Dan disliked to promote to spend more time to do more job duties.

Even, his salary would not be increased and his rank would be promoted in this moment. After six months, Dan had his job proficiently and who was quite talented and the job did not present a strong challenge to him. During to Frances, compensation director for Puma corporation recognized Dan's talent and wanted him to evaluate Puma corporation's complete benefits package for the purpose of making needed changes without the help of costly outside consultants and Frances believed that Puma's benefits package was outdated and needed to be revised. However, Frances felt Dan disliked to discuss with her to evaluate the total benefits package from her several encouraging because Dan seemed to be constantly thinking of and discussing his outdoor activities and he seemed lack of commitment to do his job. As ERG theory indicated that a person's existence needs don't necessarily have to be satisfied before who can became concerned about whose relationships with others or about using whose personal capabilities, whose desire to meet the existence needs may be stronger than whose desire to meet the two other types of needs, such as relationship with others or about using those personal capabilities, but the other needs may still be important. As this case, Dan , this company 's benefits administrator who chose to serve this company, instead of salary was paid well reason, the other reason was his job was located to let him to enjoy the outdoors sport activities conveniently. Hence, it is Dan's existence needs in this company. Hence, even Frances , this company compensation director accepted to increase Dan's salary to promote him to do higher rank after six months, due to Dan's personal capabilities was very good. Dan whose behaviour performance disliked to discuss with Frances to evaluate and Dan seemed to be constantly thinking of and discussing his outdoor activities and he seemed lack of commitment to his job. As ERG theory indicated Dan could not motivated by Frances because Frances needed him to forgive to enjoy his outdoor sport entertainment when Frances needed him to spend much time to discuss with her to evaluate the total benefits package at this moment. However, Dan felt the reason of his existence was staying in this company was because his new job could located in Utah to always enjoyed the outdoor entertainment. If he could not spend extra time to enjoy this kind of entertainment. It would cause Dan lost commitment to serve this employer.

suggestion of solvable method:

Using ERG theory, explain the reasons for the situation described in the case.

ERG theory suggests people are motivated by three hierarchically ordered types of needs: existence needs (E), relatedness needs (R) and growth needs (G). A person may work at the same time, although satisfying lower order needs often takes place before a person is strongly motivated by higher level needs.Work motivation and job satisfaction means the relationship between the organization and its members is influenced by what motivates them to work and the rewards and fulfilment they derive from it. Motivation is typified as an individual phenomenon. Every person is unique and all the major theories of motivation allow for this uniqueness to be demonstrated in one way or another, it is as intentional to assume to be under the worker's control and behaviours that are influenced by motivation, such as effort expended. Motivation is through an understanding of internal cognitive processes, that is what people feel and how who think. This understanding should help the manager to predict likely behaviour of staff in given situations. The two factors of greatest importance are what gets people activated and the force of an individual to engage in desired behaviour (direction or choice of behaviour). The purpose of motivation theories is predict behaviour. Motivation isn't the behaviour itself and it is not performance. Motivation concerns action and the internal and external forces which influence a person's choice of action.

Maslow's hierarchy of needs theory suggests people are motivated by their desire to satisfy specific needs and that needs are arranged in a hierarchy with physiological needs at the bottom and self actualization needs at the top. People most satisfy needs at lower levels before being motivated by needs at higher levels. However, ERG theory differs from Maslow's theory. Firstly, a person's existence needs don't necessarily have to be satisfied before who can become concerned about whose relationships with others or about using whose personal capabilities, whose desire to meet the existence needs may be stronger than whose desire to meet the two other types of needs, such as relationship with others or about using those personal capabilities, but the other needs may still be important. Otherwise, the need hierarchy theory proposes that the hierarchy is fixed and that physiological needs must be largely satisfied before other needs become important. Hence, using ERG theory to apply to this case, it may explain why Don Coggin did these behaviour. Although, Frances Mead , compensation director for Puma corporation , who paid well to hire Don Coggin to fill position of benefits administrator for her company in corporate personnel department at Puma, headquartered in Salt Lake city, Utah and the job was located in Utah. Hence, Don could always enjoyed the outdoor and he liked to backpack, camp and did some mountain climbing sport entertainment conveniently. Hence, it ensured that this job location could give Dan to enjoy his likely mountain climbing ,camp, backpack sport entertainment conveniently was also an important reason to influence Don to choose this job.In fact, Dan's financial background aided him greatly in his new benefits administrator job, where he was responsible for development and administration of the pension plan, life and health insurance package, employee stock purchase plan and other employee benefit programs within one month. Dan has learned how to do duties. Frances Mead, she was satisfied with her selection for Dan to do this benefits administrator position. Hence, she expected Dan to move up to in the department rank rapidly, but Dan only concern was that who did not seem to have enough time to enjoy his outdoor activities after he had seem promoted to do further duties absolutely. It implied that Dan disliked to promote to spend more time to do more job duties.

Even, his salary would not be increased and his rank would be promoted in this moment. After six months, Dan had his job proficiently and who was quite talented and the job did not present a strong challenge to him. During to Frances, compensation director for Puma corporation recognized Dan's talent and wanted him to evaluate Puma corporation's complete benefits package for the purpose of making needed changes without the help of costly outside consultants and Frances believed that Puma's benefits package was outdated and needed to be revised. However, Frances felt Dan disliked to discuss with her to evaluate the total benefits package from her several encouraging because Dan seemed to be constantly thinking of and discussing his outdoor activities and he seemed lack of commitment to do his job. As ERG theory indicated that a person's existence needs don't necessarily have to be satisfied before who can became concerned about whose relationships with others or about using whose personal capabilities, whose desire to meet the existence needs may be stronger than whose desire to meet the two other types of needs, such as relationship with others or about using those personal capabilities, but the other needs may still be important. As this case, Dan , this company 's benefits administrator who chose to serve this company, instead of salary was paid well reason, the other reason was his job was located to let him to enjoy the outdoors sport activities conveniently. Hence, it is Dan's existence needs in this company. Hence, even Frances , this company compensation director accepted to increase Dan's salary to promote him to do higher rank after six months, due to Dan's personal capabilities was very good. Dan whose behaviour performance disliked to discuss with Frances to evaluate and Dan seemed to be constantly thinking of and discussing his outdoor activities and he seemed lack of commitment to his job. As ERG theory indicated Dan could not motivated by Frances because Frances needed him to forgive to enjoy his outdoor sport entertainment when Frances needed him to spend much time to discuss with her to evaluate the total benefits package at this moment.

However, Dan felt the reason of his existence was staying in this company was because his new job could located in Utah to always enjoyed the outdoor entertainment. If he could not spend extra time to enjoy this kind of entertainment. It would cause Dan lost commitment to serve this employer. Hence, as ERG theory indicated that Dan felt he and Frances relationship would become worse and he would feel this company was not to be valued for whom to grow further and Dan would plan to leave current employer possibly if Frances continue to force Dan to discuss with her to evaluate the total benefits package for her employer. Moreover, ERG theory also indicated that when a need is satisfied, it may remain the dominant motivator if the next need in the hierarchy can't be satisfied. As Dan , benefits administrator who had satisfied whose relatedness needs to Frances, as Frances had believed who was satisfied with her selection to do this benefits administrator position absolutely within this six months. Basically, Dan felt his existence needs was satisfied with Frances, compensation director relationship. Hence, during Dan was stilling doing this benefits administration position within these six months, it might remain Dan to be this company dominant motivator, even, he could not promote to do higher rank and he could earn higher salary from Frances after these six months. In result, Dan's performance began to be poor after six months, e.g. complaints from employees regard errors and time delays in insurance claims and stock purchases began to increase. Also, Dan was package and thus no progress in the design of new benefit programs and he began to call in sick occasionally. Interestingly, he seemed to be sick on Friday and Monday, allowing for a three day weekend. It was obvious that Dan had the ability to perform the job and even more challenging tasks. In conclusion, Dan changed his behaviour and performance poorly in this company because Dan felt not he had existence needs, as he needed to spend time to discuss with Frances to evaluate the total benefits package employees, she could not let him to have more extra time to enjoy his sport entertainment as well as Dan, benefits administrator and Frances, compensation director both co-operation relationship was broken because the reason of Frances needed Dan to spend much time to discuss with her to evaluate Puma corporation's completion benefits package for the purpose of making needed changes was that she did not without the help of costly outside consultants and Frances was still not ensuring to increase his salary, she was examining Dan's ability in this stage. Hence, Frances's decision would cause Dan lost existence needs and relatedness needs and growth needs in this company. Due to these needs had been found to decrease to Dan as they were not satisfied and the lesser needs were not satisfied and the lesser are desired . Hence, it would cause Dan's behaviour and performance to be poor because Frances could not motivate Dan to get these psychological needs absolutely in this company after six months.

Using expectancy theory, explain the reasons for the situation.

Expectancy theory suggests motivation is a function of an individuals expectancy that a given amount of effort will lead to particular level of performance and judgement that indicates performance will lead to certain outcomes. Expectancy is the subjective probability that a given amount of effort will lead to a particular level of performance. Hence, manager needs to consider the factor of probability that a given amount of effort will lead to a particular level of performance and the second factor individuals consider is the perceived connection between a particular level of performance and important outcomes and the third factor is the importance of each anticipated outcome.Hence, it means individual may have different goals or needs and individual may have different connections between actions and achievement of goals to consider alternatives, weigh cost and benefit and choose action of maximum utility. Different reward can be given to individual as a result of effort or performance. Hence, expectancy theory indicates that people are influences by the expected results of their actions.

Concept of motivation is some driving force within individuals by which they attempt to achieve some goal in order to fulfil some need or expectation. People's behaviours are determined by what motivates them.Their performance is a product of both ability level and motivation. Motivation is a function of the relationship between effort expended and perceived level of performance and the expectation that rewards (desired outcomes) will be related to performance and the expectation that rewards (desired outcomes) are available. Motivation includes extrinsic and intrinsic two kind of motivations. Extrinsic motivation is related to tangible rewards such as salary and benefits, security, promotion, contract of service, the work environment and conditions of work as well as intrinsic motivation is related to psychological rewards, such as the opportunity to use one's ability, a sense of challenge and achievement, receiving appreciation, positive recognition and being treated in a caring and considerate manner.People are capable and willing to perceive fairness in their immediate environment, compare input , ability, skill, age, education, effort and training to outcome like monetary reward, praise, status, improved promotion opportunities to compare reward to others. It implies needs and expectations of staffs at work, it includes economic rewards, social relationships, intrinsic satisfaction. Hence, motivation is as psychological forces that determine the direction of a person's behaviour in an organization and a person's level of effort and a person's level of persistence. It is important that managers attempt to reduce potential frustration, for example, through, effective

recruitment, selection and socialisation, training and development, job design and work organization, equitable human resource management policies, recognition and reward, effective communications,participative styles of management, attempting to understand the individual's perception of the situation. Proper attention to motivation and to the needs and expectation of people at work will help overcome boredom and frustration induced behaviour.

To apply this expectancy theory to this case study. In fact, Dan who had lack effort and motivation to do this benefits administrator position from Frances after six months, so Dan should choose to perform whose normal job duties poorly. e.g. complaints from employees regarding errors and time delays in insurance claims and stock purchases began to increase. Even, Dan was making no progress in the evaluation of benefit package and thus no progress in the design of new benefit programs and he began to call in sick occasionally. Interestingly, he seemed to be sick on Friday and Monday, allowing for a three day weekend. It was obvious that Dan had the ability to perform the job and even more challenging tasks.The expectancy theory could explain reasons why Dan's behaviour and performance was became poor. Due to expectancy theory suggests motivation is a function of an individual's expectancy that a given amount of effort will lead a particular level of performance and judgement that indicates performance will lead to certain outcomes. Before the six months, Frances could give motivation to Dan, such as she could give good salary and good job location to satisfy Dan's life needs and outdoor sport entertainment needs and Dan and Frances both felt this job's working hours and Dan's ability and performance was very reasonable.

However, after six months, Frances needed Dan to spend much time to discuss with her to evaluate the total benefits package for her employees, but Frances could not tell Dan to ensure to increase Dan's salary and promotion after Dan should finish this extra evaluation job duties with Frances. Even, Dan felt who could not enjoy this outdoor sport entertainment due to he needed to spend much time to discuss with Frances about the total benefits package evaluation to whose employees issue. Hence,Dan would felt that who spent much effort to do this job, but he could not get fair salary and position . It would cause him to decide to change his job performance and personal behaviour to be poor , e.g. complaints from employees regarding, errors and time delays in insurance claims and stock purchases began to increase. Even, Dan was also making no progress in the evaluation of benefit package and this no progress in the design of new benefit programs and he began to call in sick occasionally. Interestingly, he seemed to be sick on Friday and Monday, allowing for a three day weekend. It was obvious that Dan had the ability (effort) to perform to job (benefit administrator position) in this Puma corporation company, but he chose to perform to do this position poorly. The reason was because Dan had judged that his expectancy was not reasonable from Frances demand because Dan needed to spend much time to discuss with Frances and who could not get higher salary and higher rank and who could not have extra time to enjoy his outdoor entertainment. Hence, Dan's decision to make poor performance and bad behaviour, his aim was to make Frances felt who had ability to change another new job possibly. Unless, Frances could change her decision not needed Dan to spend much time to discuss with her to deal this extra job duties. Otherwise, who would find another new job possibly. It implied Dan's job expectancy was not same to Frances's performance need expectancy to Dan to cause Dan's poor performance occurred after six month.

Using the integration framework found in the last major section of the chapter, describe what actions Frances should and should not take.

In fact, Dan Coggin, benefits administrator, whose behaviour performance indicated that who chose to do this job because he felt be well paid and this job was located in Utah to always enjoy the outdoors activities of backpack, camp and do some mountain climbing. Before six months, Dan's job performance was satisfied with Frances, compensation director, so it caused Dan expected Dan to move up in the department ranks rapidly . Due to Frances felt Puma's benefits package was outdated and needed to revised and who proposed to making needed changes, without the help of costly outside consultants. Thus, Frances decided to recognize Dan's talents and wanted him spent extra time to evaluate with her to discuss how Puma corporation's complete benefits package to make changed to satisfy Puma's employees benefits of needs. However, after six months, Dan's performance and behaviour began to be poor, e.g. complaints from employees regarding errors and time delays in insurance claims and stock purchase began to increase. Also, Dan was making no progress in the evaluation of benefit package and thus no progress in the design of new benefit programs and he began to call in sick occasionally. Interestingly, he seemed to be sick on Friday and Monday, allowing for a three day weekend. It was obvious that Dan had the ability to perform the job and even more challenging tasks.

However, why Dan became lazy and who disliked to spend extra time to discuss with Frances to evaluate how to change Puma corporation's complete benefits package to its employees. It was obvious that Frances forced Dan to spend extra time to discuss with her to do evaluation issue that who did not enquire Dan's desire(ideas) whether who liked or disliked to do this issue and Dan would feel who would not have time to enjoy his sport activities in this job Utah location and who also felt it was unfair to him why whose salary was not increased and position was not promoted when Dan needed to spend extra time to do extra job unreasonably.

I shall use integration framework to find whether what Frances Mead, compensation director should take actions and should not take actions. On the one hand, Frances should take these actions as below:

In common, formulating strategies that can deliver competitive advantage is not easy. Senior managers needed to work with other individuals engage in meetings, experiments, discussion and analyses in order to create or modify company strategies. Implementing strategies and engaging in the day-to-day behaviours that help to create competitive advantage also are not easy task. Hence, staffs must be motivated if who are to effectively engage in the behaviours and practices that bring advantage and success to a firm. Hence, Frances mead, compensation director should need to choose to use different strategies to require different types of people (staffs) and behaviours and therefore different approaches to motivation. To fully motivate such Dan, benefits administrator staff, resource for trying new ideas, must be available, including time and opportunities to develop new skills to change old pension plan, life and health insurance package, employee stock purchase plan and other employee benefit programs benefit package. I believe human resources and time was not enough to Frances and Dan two people to evaluate this issue. Frances ought to enquire Dan's idea whether Dan felt what cause whose performance began to be poor, e.g. complaints from employee regarding errors and time delays in insurance claims and stock purchase began to increase. To investigate whether Dan felt the issue of evaluation Puma corporation's complete benefits package issue with her or other factors that was influenced to his normal job performance to be poor. The benefits were that Frances could let Dan to tell what the reasons were to cause his performance poor honestly and their conservation could let Dan felt France could spend extra time to consider to discuss whether what Dan felt needs and dissatisfaction to cause Dan's performance poorly. Hence, Frances could judge whether Dan's ability could deal to evaluate Puma corporation's complete benefits package and this issues could not influence Dan's daily normal job duties for this benefits administrator position or not. If Frances should prefer to spend extra time to discuss with Dan about what difficulty and needs and dissatisfaction who felt to cause whose job performance began to be poor. Frances should know whether it was job factors or other factors were influenced to Dan to feel dissatisfaction to cause whose performance poorly to let Frances to revise whose strategies. The factors could include such as, unreasonable market salary, poor working environment, increasing job responsibilities and feeling difficulties, lacking opportunity for advancement or promotion, challenging work and potential for personal growth, lacking personal commitment and recognition and achievement needs to this position,lacking work and life balance needs, unreasonable company policies and working conditions and administration procedures, poor interpersonal relationship with peer and poor status security issues.

As goal setting theory suggests challenging and specific goals increase human performance because whose effort and persistence attention can be committed to affect motivation. Due to Frances didn't indicate clear specific goals to let Dan to know whether how and what steps who should use to evaluate Dan's ability to judge whose job performance was achieved to goal to promote higher rank before Dan began to do this job. Hence, Dan should feel doubt why Frances needed him to spend extra time to evaluate with Frances about making changes to Puma corporation's complete benefits package issue after six months. Hence, Frances should need to explain why who needed Dan to spend extra time to evaluate with him and they also needed to discuss further issue for this evaluation report job of about how difficult Dan felt his performance goal should be achieved whether the goal should be easy, moderately difficult or very difficult to achieve to Dan's ability, how the expert outcome should be specific or goals could be more do best what Dan needed to make commitment to achieve this goal; to what extent of feedback needs Dan should be informed of their report in this evaluation progress toward his performance goal. Hence, if Frances could let Dan to know what Dan needed to perform to achieve. Frances goal to evaluate Dan's ability clearly. Then, Dan's could judge whether Frances was a right employer for his continue staying or leaving further decision. An understanding for the factors that motivate workers are critical not only to corporate executive who concentrate on the bottom line, but more importantly to the security of companies as it relates to compete in the global market. However, the internal process view that motivation needs that activate, guide, and motivate behaviour (especially goal directed behaviour) is one of the most important concerns of modern organizational managers , as Frances Mead, compensation director for Puma corporation. The traditional motivator for a worker is his salary, but in many cases that isn't enough. As Puma corporation, Frances Mead, compensation director, it implied to use only material rewards to motivate Dan, benefits administrator staff , it was not enough and it needed to use only motivators to satisfy Dan's needs. Supposing to Dan's tasks such as development and administration of pension plan, life and health insurance and employee stock purchase package etc duties whose solution was obvious extrinsic motivators, e.g. increasing salary reward were working as which should be increase performance, but for task whose solution were more complex, such as revision and evaluation of complete outdated benefits package for the purpose how to make needed changes, extrinsic motivation should have negative effects on performance to Dan. Hence, if the task was complex, the motivation users must be intrinsic e.g. achievement, chance, promotion to give to Dan employee. Due to revision and evaluation of complete outdated benefits package was one complex and if also needed to spend more resources and time discussion tasks for Puma corporation. Hence, Frances should ought to tell Dan who should use job with performance related pay to attract him of higher ability and induced who to provide greater effort. Frances should focuses on Dan's role as an incentive system. Hence, Frances should consider compensation as a return for Dan's services rendered and saw Dan's performance was as a reflection of whose personal worth in terms of skills and abilities as well as whose education and training also had acquired. However, Frances should view compensation from two perspectives: as a major expense and as a possible influence on Dan's attitudes and behaviours through compensation based motivational strategies. This potential to influence Dan's work attitudes and behaviours and subsequently the productivity and effectiveness of Puma corporation.

Attribute theory indicated that when an outcome, such as poor performance is attributed to a stable cause. such as low intelligence, it is logical to expect that the employee's performance isn't going to change in the future. If the same poor performance is attributed to a less stable factor, such as insufficient effort, a employer can expect that the employee could improve whose performance by working harder in the future. Thus, Frances should consider what attributions were to influence Dan's job performance began to be poor, then who should revise whose actions should be changed to solve this issue. The attribution should influence Dan's performance to be poor, internal and stable attribution, such as whether Dan's intelligence could deal his normal job duties and extra job duties of evaluation on Puma's benefits package both at the same time; external and unstable attribution, such as whether Dan had enough effort and time to attempt to discuss with Frances to finish this extra job duties of

evaluation on Puma's benefits package within limited time or external and unstable attribution, such as whether Frances' temporary strategy or decision was without the help of outside consultants to evaluate Puma's benefits package whether which should give pressure or effort to Dan to attempt to help him to finish this evaluation job, it meant that Dan would do this duties, even which should also influence whose normal duties to be poor if Dan felt pressure to attempt to do this extra duties. Frances should need to provide feedback to Dan about whose progress toward performance goals was well established . In fact, feedback on performance was likely to have a positive effect on motivation. Moreover, Dan's feedback was important when benefits package of evaluation of performance goals existed and when Dan was relatively difficult to achieve. Hence, Frances's feedback should encourage Dan to discover (find) errors to know what he should need to improve during evaluation was progressing and Frances should not have due date limitation to let Dan felt pressure to finish this benefit plan evaluation job ,even if influenced to whose normal job duties poorly .

Expectancy theory provides a useful framework for organizing those factors : people will be committed to goals that carrying a reasonable expectation of being attained and are more viewed as desirable to attain. Frances should judge whether human resource inputs were enough to do this benefit package evaluation job with Dan. It was possible that Dan felt human resource inputs were out enough to cause who felt pressure to attempt to dot this extra job duties with Frances and Dan should feel inequity and unfair treatment and unreasonable due to who should need to spend extra time to do this extra evaluation job with Frances. Hence,

Frances should need to explain to let Dan to know why who needed Dan to attempt to do this extra evaluation job as well as what benefits were Dan should give reward if Dan's evaluation job performance could satisfy Frances' requirement. Then Dan would be committed to goals that carrying a reasonable expectation of being attained and was more viewed as desirable to attain. On the other hand, Frances should not take these actions as below: Although Dan performance began to become poor after six months due to Dan needed to spend extra time to discuss with Frances to evaluate how to change Puma corporation old benefits package issue. However, Frances should not angry to blame Dan immediately. The reason was that Dan's performance was still good before six months. It meant that who had ability to do this position.Hence, Dan ought have ability to assist Frances to evaluate the changed needs to current benefits package evaluation to Puma corporation's employees with Frances discussion together.

Otherwise, if Frances should blame to Dan. it would cause Dan felt Frances was not a good compensation director to manage and co-operate with him to work together and it was possible that would choose to leave Puma corporation to find any employer immediately. Then, Frances would feel difficult to spend more time to choose applicants to re-employ another new staff to do this benefit administrator position, instead of Dan and Frances should also need to spend more time to train this new staff. Hence, Frances should not blame Dan. Otherwise, Frances should need to enquire why Dan's performance to be poor whether Dan's poor performance behaviour was caused by extra evaluation job duties factor or other personal factors to revise Dan's errors to expect Dan to continue to assist Frances to finish this evaluation job effectively and efficiently.

In conclusion, I did not agree Frances, compensation director should blame Dan immediately because Dan believed himself had owned market competitive ability due to Dan had worked in Puma corporation six months . It should give Dan had confidence to change another new employer if Dan felt Frances' personal attitude was not friendly to arrange any further new jobs to him to do. Hence, Frances should enquire Dan why who performed poorly in order to solve whose personal trouble issues and then Frances should also attempt to find some methods to satisfy Dan's personal needs to motivate and persuade Dan to continue to co-operate with Frances in this company together.

CHAPTER VI

The Frontier hotel

Walt and Tony were working in the Frontier hotel, Walt was head waiter and Tony was head chef. Then, Tony encouraged Walt to start a restaurant and who promoted himself to be Walt's restaurant's head chef. Finally, after several meetings and a lot of planning, Walt and Bill decided to open a Italian restaurant and employ Tony to be head chef. After then, Walt and Bill both partners tried to encourage Tony to join them in partnership, but Tony had refused and his personal reason was to lose his freedom. However, Walt dissatisfied Tony's performance because Tony had begun waking up late for work and who had missed several shifts altogether and who also often liked to drink alcohol. Hence, Tony performed bad behaviour to cause this conflict with Walt. Although their age were late thirties years old and before they were head positions in the Frontier hotel, but Tony had personal problem, such as marriage was broken and who liked to spend much time to meet girlfriend and who often drank alcohol in his private life. Tony's private life was seemed to influence whose head chef cooking job in Walt's Italian restaurant. Although, the Italian restaurant could expand to a large location. Walt and Bill two partners could earn profit and Tony head chef could earn Frontier hotel and Italian restaurant both employers' salaries in the same time within one year. However, Tony's performance was became poor, e.g. who didn't come to work and who had called in sick to Walt. In fact, who told lie to Walt, Tony spent sick time to meet whose girlfriend. Sometime, Tony arrived Walt's restaurant to work , but sometimes who was absent. Tony had also often drunk alcohol for two years during who had worked in Frontier hotel and Italian restaurant in the period.

suggestion of solvable method:

Could Tony's problem with alcohol be stress related?

Explain why or why not?

Walt and Tony were working in the Frontier hotel, Walt was head waiter and Tony was head chef. Then, Tony encouraged Walt to start a restaurant and who promoted himself to be Walt's restaurant's head chef. Finally, after several meetings and a lot of planning, Walt and Bill decided to open a Italian restaurant and employ Tony to be head chef. After then, Walt and

Bill both partners tried to encourage Tony to join them in partnership, but Tony had refused and his personal reason was to lose his freedom. However, Walt dissatisfied Tony's performance because Tony had begun waking up late for work and who had missed several shifts altogether and who also often liked to drink alcohol. Hence, Tony performed bad behaviour to cause this conflict with Walt. Although their age were late thirties years old and before they were head positions in the Frontier hotel, but Tony had personal problem, such as marriage was broken and who liked to spend much time to meet girlfriend and who often drank alcohol in his private life. Tony's private life was seemed to influence whose head chef cooking job in Walt's Italian restaurant. Although, the Italian restaurant could expand to a large location. Walt and Bill two partners could earn profit and Tony head chef could earn Frontier hotel and Italian restaurant both employers' salaries in the same time within one year. However, Tony's performance was became poor, e.g. who didn't come to work and who had called in sick to Walt. In fact, who told lie to Walt, Tony spent sick time to meet whose girlfriend. Sometime, Tony arrived Walt's restaurant to work , but sometimes who was absent. Tony had also often drunk alcohol for two years during who had worked in Frontier hotel and Italian restaurant in the period.

I believe Tony's problem could be with alcohol stress related. I shall give these reasons as below:

Stress means a feeling of tension that occurs when a person perceives that a situation is about to exceed whose ability to cope whose ability to cope and consequently can endanger whose well being and who feels whose capabilities or resources or needs don't match the demands or requirements of the job. In fact, it was possible that Tony would feel stress because Tony was working two head chef positions in Frontier hotel and Italian restaurant at the same time. He should feel very busy to work and who could not use enough time to meet his girlfriend. Although Tony could earn double salaries from these two employers, but he felt stress after one year. Hence, after one year, Tony did poor performance (behaviour) to let Walt to know, e.g. Tony had begun waking up late for work, who had missed several shifts although. Thus, Tony's stress had poor consequences to Walt's Italian restaurant and to Tony's himself. These poor consequences followed from the effects on Tony's individual's performance that include lower motivation, dissatisfaction, low job performance, increased absenteeism and lower quality of relationships at work, increased safety risks in kitchen and increased health care and increased costs to Tony's alcohol drinking problem. Thus, stress would cause Tony's bad behavioural consequences, e.g. abusing alcohol, late work, absenteeism and Tony's individual's frequently missed work due to stress related illness personal problems. In fact, Tony needed to do two head chef cooking jobs for two employers at the same time. It would cause psychological stress to Tony, e.g. anxiety, depression, low self esteem, sleeplessness, frustration or family problems(marriage was broken). Tony's drinking alcohol problem would increase stress to influence whose job performance to be poor. It caused Tony could not wake up early to work lately, Tony would absent to work to follow shift time often and Tony could not cooperate with kitchen cookers team and waiter team easier and became increasing isolated with them. Thus, Tony's problem with alcohol influenced whose work and private times could not adopt to cause a serious source of stress related. Due to Walt's restaurant work demands had increased to Tony to need spend longer working hours, fast and short time cooking speed needs to satisfy client increasing numbers needs. The most important, Tony needed to work for head chef two jobs for Frontier hotel and Italian restaurant both employers at the sane time. Hence, Tony's work overload could be quantitative increasing too much cooking work. In conclusion, Tony's bad behavioural habit, such as abusing alcohol drinking problem could be caused to stress related due to influence his sickness, woke up late for work and lacked enough nervous and energy to do cooking job and felt not enough sleeping time. Thus abusing alcohol drinking problem was cause nervous stress to Tony's cooking job performance absolutely.

What should Walt do in this circumstance to help Tony cope?

In fact, it implied Tony would feel stress to perform those behaviours, such as who had begun waking up late for work, who had missed several shifts altogether to work to Walt and Bill two partners' Italian restaurant. Due to Tony was working Frontier hotel and Italian restaurant as two head chef positions as the same time. It was possible that Tony felt who needed to spend too much nervous and energy to do cooking job in these two employers and who needed to do shifts job duties for Walt's Italian restaurant and Frontier hotel both as well as Tony had also bad drinking alcohol habit two years, it would influence who could not have nervous to concentrate on cooking job in Walt's Italian restaurant's Kitchen. Because cooking head chef job was needed to spend too much energy (effort) and nervous and time if Tony hoped to cook good tactic foods to Walt's Italian restaurant's clients to eat and who hoped to lead his cooking team work efficiently with waiters team to provide good service to Walt restaurant clients. However, Tony had missed several shifts, it was possible that Tony preferred to spend his private time to meet whose girlfriend, who felt who spend shift time to work in Walt's

Italian restaurant which would reduce he could enjoy his private life time with her as well as Tony had begun waking up late for work, it was possible that Tony had alcohol drinking abused problem long time , it would caused Tony has serious psychological stress responses, e.g. depression, low self esteem, sleeplessness, frustration or family problems(marriage broken). The most important, although Tony could earn double salaries due to who had been working Frontier hotel and Italian restaurant both employers at the same time, but Tony would enough lack nervous and energy and who would feel difficult to adopt to arrange time to do cooking jobs with whose team efficiently. So, Tony would feel very hard to earn double salaries after Tony had begun to choose to do Walt's Italian restaurant and Frontier hotel cooking jobs at the same time after one year. However, I shall recommend that Walt should attempt to use these methods to help Tony cope in this circumstance. Workplace stress can occur when individual (Tony) perceive the demands of the workplace to outweigh whose resources for coping with those demands as well as workplace demands are aspects of the work environment that job holder (Tony head chef) must handle. Hence, Tony was current stressor but who had little control over this situation from Walt's fear authority to him. The most important, Walt should not let Tony to feel who gave more stress to Tony's cooking duties because Tony should choose to leave Walt's cooking job to serve only Frontier hotel employer or who should perform to lead whose cooking team to influence waiter team co-operation poorly and who could not cook better taste to foods to satisfy clients needs

if Walt's behaviour should let Tony to feel more stress and unhappy to work. Hence, Walt needed to use organizational stress management method to help Tony to reduce stress or helped Tony to deal more efficiently with Tony's stress. Walt could attempt to let Tony to increase his individual's autonomy and control to his working time, e.g. Tony could choose to arrange what shift working times were the most suitable to him to work every day in order to make Tony could arrange what shift times to work in Frontier hotel or Italian restaurant every day.Walt should ensure that Tony was compensated properly and maintained job demands / requirements at healthy levels to ensure that Tony had enough nervous and energy and time to prepare to cook and lead whose cooking team to co-operate with waiter team efficiently. Demand control model that suggests experienced stress is a function when demands are high , but individuals have little control over situation. The two factors can create situations of job strain and the experience of stress include the workplace demands faced by employer and the control that an individual has in meeting those demands. In fact, Tony felt pressure due to who needed to do both shift time jobs at the same time. If Walt could employ more cookers to assist Tony to do cooking job and Walt could change Tony to do part time shift job. It would reduced Tony nervous workload to do both cooking jobs and it could let Tony had more relax time to sleep. Effort reward imbalance model that suggests experienced stress is a function of both required effort and rewards obtained. Stress is highest when required effort is high but rewards are low. It focused two factors include the effort required by employer and the rewards an individual receives as a result of the effort. Hence, it was possible that Tony felt who required effort and nervous and time were high but rewards were low to work in Walt's Italian restaurant to compare to Frontier hotel employer. It implied that Walt needed to increase Tony's salary if who hoped Tony could serve whose Italian restaurant long time. Otherwise, Tony would choose to leave Walt's cooking job.

Is Tony saveable?

Do the benefits outweigh the costs of trying to save him?

Tony can be attempt to saveable to work in Walt's Italian restaurant in the one to three months probationary period to evaluate whether the benefits outweigh the cost of trying to save Tony or not save.

Effort required relates to performance demands and obligations of the jobs. It is more narrowly focused on the job itself rather than on broader aspects of the overall work environment. It indicates a combination of strong required efforts and low rewards to any employees in organization to cause whose have strong negative emotions and harmful changes. Although a individual facing such a situation could simply exist, many stay because of limited opportunities in the labour market, hope for changes in the situation and excessive work related over commitment. (it is driven by achievement , motivation and approval motivation). In fact, Tony had enough effort and cooking skill and experience to choose which hotel or restaurant employer who liked to work in this labour market. Hence, Tony felt no worry his poor behaviour to cause Walt should dismiss him. Moreover, Tony was also working head chef shift job in another hotel at the same time. So, it was possible that Tony performed absent and woke up late to work and told lie to sickness and drunk alcohol of bad behaviour that who wanted Walt knew that they ought to discuss salary rising issue. Otherwise Tony should leave Walt's employment.The reason was because Tony felt spend much effort and time and nervous to do head chef job in Walt's Italian restaurant, but Walt could not give reasonable rewards to Tony to compare Frontier hotel employer at the same time. Hence, Tony begun waking up late for work and who begun to miss several shifts after he worked one year in Walt's Italian restaurant. Hence, Tony did action to complaint Walt to imply whose dissatisfaction to Walt's employment. However, Walt could attempt to increase Tony's salary and let Tony to choose to change to do part time shift.

Even who could let Tony to choose what shift time who preferred to work and who could suggested Tony who would not spend much time to meet girlfriend and drunk alcohol , who would spend time to sleep to prepare to do cooking job every day. Walt could enquire Tony whether who needed extra cookers and assistant head chefs staffs to assist him when the restaurant was busy time. If Tony felt who lack enough cookers and assistant head chef to assist him to do cooking job in kitchen when the restaurant was busy time. Walt ought need to spend extra salaries to employ extra staffs to assist Tony. Hence, Walt needed to discuss with Tony about how to change his shift job time and whether Tony accepted full time or accepted part time shift job and whether how many extra cookers and assistance head chefs who needed . After they had negotiated successfully, Walt could begin to give one to three months probationary period to evaluate whether Tony was suitable to do whose staff or not.

In conclusion, Walt could give one to three months probationary period to evaluate(measure) whether Tony could have enough effort and nervous to continue to do this cooking job. However, if Walt felt Tony's performance was still dissatisfactory. Walt needed give final chance to Tony to chose either who didn't work full time shift head chef job in Frontier hotel or leave Walt's job immediately.

CHAPTER VII

Willard University

Frances Workman could own those above personal trait leadership characteristics to do this Willard University president job successfully. For example, Frances workman has been president of Willard University for less than two years. Frances had been an excellent speaker and used every opportunity to speak to citizen groups as well as who also worked hard to build good relationship with the major politicians and business leaders and who managed to maintain favourable relationship with most. Frances had proved to own a trait leader's personality ability, such as intelligence and verbal fluency, self confidence and interpersonal skill. Frances was an achievement drive leader, such as France could lobbied legislature and the Willard University coordinating board for a larger share of higher education budget dollars. In the result, Frances could build favourable image to efforts to increase funding for Willard University within two years, as well as Frances president, could build a positive image to people and let them to build a positive image to people and let them to build a positive image of Willard University . The results of whose efforts included an increase in enrolment of more in the last year. This occurred when most other colleges enrolments were also decreasing as well as $2 million dollars outside funds were donated to Willard University and faculty morale was higher in the first year. Hence, Frances could judge and adapt and dominance and was tolerance for stress to deal new issue to achieve this Willard University aim successfully within two years. It proved that Frances owned trait leadership style. However, Frances was seemed to be employee centre leadership style president, it meant a behavioural leadership style that emphasised employees' personal needs and the development of interpersonal relationships and a employee centre leader frequently delegated decision making authority and responsibility to others and provided a supportive environment, encouraging interpersonal communication. For example, Frances president, concentrated on handling external matters and who delegated the responsibility for daily internal operations to whose three major vice presidents. Hence, Frances could build concentrate on building positive image to public people and let them to build a positive image of Willard University. Finally,Frances could help Willard University to increase student enrolment numbers of more in the last year and $2 million outside funds were donated to Willard University and faculty morale was higher in the first year. Otherwise, this occurred when most other college enrolments were also decreasing. Thus, it proved Frances Workman leadership skill was successfully. Secondly, based on information provided, Alvin Thomas was lack trait theory of leadership style personal characteristics, who was not such as self esteem and dominance, whose ability was not such as intelligence and non verbal fluency, non judgement, non adaptability, non enthusiasm, non achievement drive, lack self confidence , non tolerance for stress and non interpersonal skill. Hence, Alvin Thomas lacked trait leadership style to do Eastern State University president successfully. For example, Alvin Thomas had been president as Eastern State University about three years, who was not as popular externally as Frances and who was not a particularly effective speaker. Hence, it proved Alvin Thomas was not a verbal fluency and lack interpersonal

skill president.

suggestion of solvable method:

Based on the information provides, describe France's and AI's leadership styles.

Leadership means the process of providing general direction and influencing individuals or groups to achieve goals. Formal leader can be formally designated by the organization or informal leader can provide leadership without such formal designation. Leader needs to lead group, team and social processes can directly or indirectly affect behaviour in organizations. The behaviour of leader has positive effects to link between leadership and organizational performance and who needs have developed a vision as well as specific goals to whose organization. Leadership styles (traits) that have been identified as important include flexibility and creativity, especially because of the importance of innovation to leader whose organization. Firstly, based on information provided, France's was belonged to trait theory of leadership style, trait leadership style includes those personality characteristics, leader was such as self esteem and dominance; leader's ability was such as intelligence and verbal fluency, judgement, adaptability, enthusiasm, achievement drive, self confidence, tolerance for stress and interpersonal skill. Frances Workman could own those above personal trait leadership characteristics to do this Willard

University president job successfully. For example, Frances workman has been president of Willard University for less than two years. Frances had been an excellent speaker and used every opportunity to speak to citizen groups as well as who also worked hard to build good relationship with the major politicians and business leaders and who managed to maintain favourable relationship with most. Frances had proved to own a trait leader's personality ability, such as intelligence and verbal fluency, self confidence and interpersonal skill. Frances was an achievement drive leader, such as France could lobbied legislature and the Willard Universitycoordinating board for a larger share of higher education budget dollars. In the result, Frances could build favourable image to efforts to increase funding for Willard University within two years, as well as Frances president, could build a positive image to people and let them to build a positive image to people and let them to build a positive image of Willard University . The results of whose efforts included an increase in enrolment of more in the last year. This occurred when most other colleges enrolments were also decreasing as well as $2 million dollars outside funds were donated to Willard University and faculty morale was higher in the first year. Hence, Frances could judge and adapt and dominance and was tolerance for stress to deal new issue to achieve this Willard University aim successfully within two years. It proved that Frances owned trait leadership style. However, Frances was seemed to be employee centre leadership style president, it meant a behavioural leadership style that emphasised employees' personal needs and the development of interpersonal relationships and a employee centre leader frequently delegated decision making authority and responsibility to others and provided a supportive environment, encouraging interpersonal communication. For example, Frances president, concentrated on handling external matters and who delegated the responsibility for daily internal operations to whose three major vice presidents. Hence, Frances could build concentrate on building positive image to public people and let them to build a positive image of Willard University. Finally,Frances could help Willard University to increase student enrolment numbers of more in the last year and $2 million outside funds were donated to Willard University and faculty morale was higher in the first year. Otherwise, this occurred when most other college enrolments were also decreasing. Thus, it proved Frances Workman leadership skill was successfully. Secondly, based on information provided, Alvin Thomas was lack trait theory of leadership style personal

characteristics, who was not such as self esteem and dominance, whose ability was not such as intelligence and non verbal fluency, non judgement, non adaptability, non enthusiasm, non achievement drive, lack self confidence , non tolerance for stress and non interpersonal skill. Hence, Alvin Thomas lacked trait leadership style to do Eastern State University president successfully. For example, Alvin Thomas had been president as Eastern State University about three years, who was not as popular externally as Frances and who was not a particularly effective speaker. Hence, it proved Alvin Thomas was not a verbal fluency and lack interpersonal
skill president.

A path goal leadership theory focuses on several types of leader behaviour and situation factors as well as Directive leadership behaviour is characterized by implementing guideline, providing information on what is expected, setting definite performance standards and ensuring individuals follow the rules. Participative leadership behaviour is characterized by sharing information, consulting with those whose who are led and emphasizing group decision making. However, Alvin Thomas was seemed to be job centre leadership style president, it emphasises employer tasks and the methods used to accomplish them. A job centre leader supervises individuals closely , provides instructions, checks frequently on performance and sometimes behaves in a punitive manner toward them. For example, who did not spend much time dealing with the external affairs of the University, who delegated much of that responsibility to one vice president. Hence, who spent much of whose time working on the internal operation of the University and less of whose time working on the external affairs. Although, who delegated much of responsibility to one vice president to assist who to do external affairs, but Eastern State University's a large number of students still without adequate faulty and it was not involved in externally funded research as well as although, who spent much time dealing with the internal operation of the University and who was committed to develop a quality University, but who did not change the administrative structure of the University within three years. He seemed to lack leadership skill. For example, who planned to give responsibility to one vice president and who had high performance expectation to them, set ambitious, goals and reviewed every significant decision made in the University and replying heavily on whose vice president to implement them effectively and who developed planning system and maintained good relations with University board. Hence, who often needed to supervise whose every vice presidents to deal external affairs closely and provided instructions, checked frequently on their every performance within those three years. But, Eastern State University student enrolment numbers declined slightly by almost 300 students and Eastern State University record was removed from American association of University professors, externally funded research had increased by approximately by $2 million dollars during the previous year, even faculty morale was declining and most faculty members did not believe who had an important voice in the administration of the University. However, who spent much of his time working on the internal operation of the University, but faculty morale was declining and most faculty members did not believe who had an important voice in the administration of the University as well as who could not lead to the one vice president and who also could not provide instructions and checked whose performance how to deal external affairs correctly. Hence, it implied that whose leadership skill was not successful within these three years.

What are the important factors that the leaders of Willard and Eastern must consider in order to be effective?

The important factors that the leaders of Willard University and Eastern State University must consider in order to be effective as below:

The Eastern State University president, Alvin Thomas both were as their organizations' chief executive officers who were very important given the substantial influence design Universities strategies and overseeing Universities' implementation to lead their vice presidents to deal internal or external affairs efficiently and effectively. Frances Workman and Alvin Thomas both presidents needed to develop a vision for their Universities' units or groups led, who also needed to manage Universities limited resources under their direction to include financial capital, but especially human capital, e.g. vice president and administrator position numbers and who also needed to build valuable interpersonal relationships (social capital) with University staffs and good University images (goodwill) to let current and future students and parents to fell those two Universities goodwill existed in global education market. Hence, both Willard University and Eastern State University both presidents needed to provide effective leadership that could enhance associates productivity, e.g. Improving lecturers' teaching methods and skills and improving office administrators and service staffs whose service performance to manage human capital well and built and maintained relationships both with whose Universities' different organizations(departments) with internal associates and other leaders ,e.g. vice presidents and externally with alliance partners and colleges and universities.Those two university presidents ought need to criticize if their universities didn't meet their goals or their university teams have a losing reason. Hence, these two university presidents needed to revise their performance to find why their universities could not achieve their goals and they needed to discuss any meetings to attempt to find any solutions from university boards every year.These two university presidents (leaders) needed to provide direction and to influence all universities staffs during who begun to do their new jobs and during who were doing their new jobs, who needed to attempt to do these activities effectively, e.g. providing useful information (guidelines) to assist vice presidents how to carry on dealing their external and internal affairs, resolving conflicts, motivating followers, anticipating problems, developing mutual respect among groups (university departments)members and coordinating groups (departments) activities and efforts. It aimed to revise what presidents do activities were not effective and then they could know what activities who needed to change to discuss with vice presidents to find solutions more effectively.These two university presidents also needed to build leader member relations, it meant the degree to which a leader was respected and was accepted as a leader and had friendly interpersonal relations. If these two presidents could build friendly interpersonal relations to their colleges, such as vice presidents, administrators etc senior staffs. It would increase these staffs confidence and assistance to these two presidents further the years. Thus, if these two universities' presidents could attempt to change their management attitude to their colleagues (staffs), special senior position staffs, then I believed that they could lead their universities' different teams (departments) to work more effectively. In fact, not all people in positions that call for leader behaviour, e.g. management positions. A manager who follows rules and fails to provide direction to and support for whose associates is not acting as a leader.The measuring the effectiveness of leaders factors include productivity, job satisfaction, absenteeism, turnover rates of staffs being led. Thus, the presidents of these two universities needed to consider how to lead whose staffs to work effectively in order to achieve their universities' aim every year. Otherwise, these two presidents would be only a manager role who only followed universities' rules to work, but who did not provided direction to and supported to their associates effectively. Hence, who would not acting as a leader role. Any leaders who need have leadership traits characteristics include that driver refers

to the amount ambition; leadership motivation refers to a person's desire to lead and influence others; assuming responsibility; leaders with honesty are truthful what they say and what they do; leaders must be confident in their actions and showing that confidence to other; leaders who posses a high degree of intelligence are better able to process complex information and deal with changing environments and these two presidents(leaders) of this two universities needed to prepare management knowledge of the domain in which who were engaged allows who to make better decisions and prepared to anticipate future their universities internal and

external issues and understood the implications of their colleges, e.g. vice president actions easily.

Compare and contrast France's and AI's effectiveness as leaders of their respective Universities .

In fact, Willard University president Frances Workman ,whose leadership was more effective than Eastern State University president Alvin Thomas performance. The reasons were that Frances had worked in Willard University for less than two year, who could deal external issues and internal structure of the organization, administrative component effectively. For example, Frances had started a new alumni club to help finance academic needs, such as new library facilities and higher salaries for faculty and staff successfully. In addition, who lobbies legislative and the university coordinating board for a larger share of higher education budget dollars. In the result, her favourable image to efforts to increase funding for Willard University. Frances could concentrate on handling external matters and who delegated the responsibility for internal operations to her three major vice presidents.However, before Frances arrival, this university had several presidents, but none of whom could manage university's internal affairs effectively. Due to the lack of leadership resulted in low faculty morale, which affected student enrolment to cause university had a poor public image. Otherwise, after Frances arrival, who could build a positive image to people and let them to build a positive image of Willard University. The results of whose efforts include an increase in enrolment of more in the last year. This occurred when other colleges enrolments were also decreasing. Hence, Willard University had a serious competition to it's competitors and $2 million dollars outside funds were donated to Willard

University and faculty morale were higher in the first year. Otherwise, another Eastern State university, had Alvin Thomas as president who had been president about three years longer than France's working period and who was not as popular externally as Frances, who was not a particularly effective speaker and did not spend much time dealing with the external affairs of the university, who delegated much of that responsibility to one vice president, who did work with external groups but in a quieter may than Frances did and who spent much of his time working on the internal operation of the university. However, who led this university poorly and the Eastern State University had these problems which included a large number of students without adequate faculty; it was not involved in externally funded research. Although, who was committed to develop a quality university, but who did not change the internal operational administrative structure of this university from his one vice president successfully. In fact, State University still had more students than Willard University, but its student enrolment

declined slightly by almost 300 students after Alvin Thomas started to manage this university. Although, Alvin Thomas had high performance expectations to staffs, set ambitious goals and reviewed every significant decision made in the university and replying heavily on whose one vice president to implement them effectively and who developed planning system and maintained good relations with university board. However, State University record was removed from American association of university professors, although, externally funded research had increased by approximately $2 million dollars only during whose three years working periods; but faculty morale was declining and most faculty members did not believe who had an important voice in the administration of the university. Hence, Alvin Thomas who could not lead faculty staffs built confidence to continue to serve this university and who could not raise public had confident its lecturers whose educational quality and performance.

What did each do well?

The Willard University president, Frances Workman who performed more well to compare another Eastern State University president, Alvin Thomas as below:

France had performed as an excellent speaker and used every opportunity to speak to citizen groups as well as who also worked hard to build good relationship with the major politicians and business leaders and who managed to maintain favourable relationship with most. Hence, who could build favourable image to efforts to increase funding for Willard University within two years. Frances knew whose strengths, so who concentrated on handling external matters and who delegated the responsibility for daily internal operations to whose three major vice presidents.

In conclusion, who was an effective leader to lead three vice presidents and the student numbers were also increasing largely and Willard University and faculty morale was higher in the first year during Frances had worked in the university within two years.

The Eastern State University president, Alvin Thomas could not perform well within three years. Although,who did not spend much time dealing with the external affairs of the university and who delegated much of that responsibility to one vice president to deal external affairs, so who could spend much of whose time

working on the internal operations and less of whose time working on external affairs. However, Eastern State University's a large number of students still without adequate faculty and it was not involved in externally funded research and who did not change the administrative structure during Alvin had worked in the university three years. In the result, student enrolment numbers declined slightly by almost 300 students and university record was removed from American association of university professors, even faculty morale was declining and most faculty numbers did not believe who had an important voice in the administration of the university. Hence, who only knew how to delegate to give responsibility to only one vice president to deal internal operations and who concentrated on dealing external affairs alone. However, externally funded research had increased by approximately by $2 million dollars during the previous year. In conclusion, Alvin Thomas could not lead whose teams to deal external affairs and internal operations effectively to compare to Frances Workman, who only helped university to give funded research $2 million amount increased, but who could not build good university image and raised department administration efficiency effectively within these three year.

What could each have done to be more effective?

I should recommend these methods to raise these both university presidents Alvin and Frances whose leadership who each could have done to be more effectively. It would be divided internal operations and external affairs two aspects:

On the dealing external affairs hand, they needed have clear external marketing and communication strategic plan. It aimed to create marketing, communication and branding strategies that maximize demand for these two universities' degree course programs to persuade many external parties (donors) to donate more to support them. First, they could oversee the editorial direction, design and production of all publications, universities web properties, social media initiatives, advertising and media with a goal of creating dynamic and engaging materials that reflected the key brand attributed of these both universities.Second, they needed to lead crisis and issues management planning and rapid response messaging to deal strategic counsel on reputation and issues management to senior leadership.

Third, they needed set strategy for marketing, communication, advertising and promotions to ensure that all messages from their universities were accurate, consistent and presented a image and they needed to built partner with university leaderships to generate innovative ideas and solutions to engage donors. Fourth, they needed to oversee the development and execution of their strategies for their universities' interactive and social media programs and supervised the development and deployment of web/ social media sites aimed at enhancing their universities' brands and reputation as well as they needed to lead a diverse team of web producers, graphic designers, project managers, marketing and editorial writers, media specialists to provide mentorship to staffs both in terms of departmental strategies. Aimed to increase donation chances and student numbers for long term.Fifth, they needed to cultivate strong working relationships with staff faculty and students across their universities and they also needed to raise the value of the Willard University and Eastern State University and effective studying market to present whose universities' history (stories) to know.They could attempt to use these communication medias (channels), social media e.g. university magazines, radio or television advertisements and other forms of digital communication. Proven success at developing and implementing online and social media strategies to enhance visibility and engagement and loyalty.The most important, their vice presidents also needed to appreciate for their universities' history, achievement and aspirations of Willard and Eastern State Universities and the ability to effectively articulate whose presidents' vision to diverse external audiences as well as who also needed to have ability to synthesize complex information and produced marketing and communication materials that addressed a wide variety of goals and objectives as well as they also needed to have excellent judgement and creative problems and solving skills including negotiation and conflict resolution as well as who also needed have confidence to project credibility to the media and other strategic stakeholders.Moreover, these two university presidents needed to prepare enough resources to provide, e.g. strategies, media communication channel, excellent leadership skill and effective human resources. The, these two presidents(leaders) could have more ability to attempt to perform more effective for their job duties.

These two universities presidents' fundraising responsibilities were creation and communication of a vision for their universities. Thus, they should temper whose ideas and goals to match the overall fundraising potential of their universities. The fund donors wanted to know about their presidents' vision and their universities; strategic direction along with the resources their universities needed to get.

Conversations between these presidents and prospective major donors and who would focus on what the donors wanted whose gift to accomplish. It is important to listen to the donors rather than drive hard. Fundraising included not only such factors as having a clear vision for these two universities and strategic priorities that would be reason with prospective donors and afforded sufficient fundraising potential, but also possessing a professional staff with the expertise and budget to get job along and a commitment was from the president of their time and energy to lead the campaign to successful completion. Seeking external fundraising counsel was often very useful to these two universities. Hence, these two presidents should also recognize that the long term nature of donor relationships was that who existed between the donor and their universities, not with these two presidents personally due to these presidents, academic deans, faculty members and professional fundraising staffs were agents role acting on behalf of their universities. On the dealing internal operational affairs hand, If these two university presidents were going to spend most of their time leading, then who needed to recruit others to do the managing. They needed to put together a group of managers to every university departments, e.g. administration, marketing and communication, finance and accounting ,student service, education etc departments. It aimed to let every department had a manager (leader) to lead their teams to adopt every department sudden changing in any time. After appointed these staffs, they must be delegated to deal as much of the problem solving. Moreover, their universities' committee chairing also needed to be delegated to avoid to deal extra internal operations with detail and caused to have too little time to perform the key function of setting the target and motivating people for their main duties. To lead change successfully, these both university presidents needed an effective decision making structure that could respond rapidly to internal and external affairs and pressures. It meant making the decision making

structures needed to become less hierarchal and complex. Many changes were failure because the vision and the strategies were not adequately communicated to the staffs to get whose commitment and support to achieve organizational success effectively.They also needed effective communication strategy for their universities, normal methods of communication,internal newspapers, meetings with deans and heads of universities which were all important. Moreover, they also needed to visit other universities and departments regularly, held informal meetings with small groups of senior staffs, recruits and other natural groupings.These two universities also needed to considerate how to evaluate staff performance to compensate them to feel fairly.The new systems of appraisal method, including 360 degree assessment for senior management and promotion which together linked the work of individuals much more directly to their key university objectives also be needed to be achieve. So, these two universities needed to appraise individuals and units and vice presidents were needed to motivate by recognising and rewarding achievement and who were not compensated not only by praise and status but also by money and these two universities also needed to allocate resources which would always be scare to units and to individuals on a performance related basis.Assuming to these two universities academic were responsible for academic affairs when their presidents and administration practiced a centralized management of all resources and planning decision, it meant that their universities' departments needed to share and allocate their duties clearly. So, new ways were needed to facilitate this process of change possible and to avoid the risk.

The introduction of a supportive evaluation system, aiming at identifying not only areas of excellence, but critical situations as well, in order to get possible solutions for their whole universities' departments as well as the introduction of a new goal oriented approach in administration and the linkage of the expansion of the administrative staffs to goals.I suggested that their universities' organizations of the administrative structure needed a clear definition of functions and responsibilities to match the newly focussed objectives and general development plans, such as there would be no faculties, but quite large academic departments whose heads would report to vice presidents directly. Hence, university heads needed to change their duties, as the vice president was responsible for academic affairs and external relations as well as the chef executives (presidents) was responsible for finance, human resources and other internal management activities. For example, one of the largest tasks was to devise a combined programme of undergraduate and postgraduate courses.It was also necessary to plan and implemented new administration systems for finance, human resources, student records, libraries, computer systems websites etc. It meant that these would be in overlap of some services and staffs. It was decided that the new reorganizations would have two heads for an interim period

and to follow a process, e.g. offering job sharing or alternative jobs to staffs displaced. It aimed to reduce their universities' expenditures. They then had to be challenged to consider realistically what the new department should become, what was needed to make that new vision become reality and what might need to realise the vision and ensured it made an impact externally. The reason of this new vision needed to be considered immediately was that it provided a structure, a focus to planning and stopped development where staffs were focus on the negative aspects of change. There was a range of internal and external relationships that had to be managed reorganization. If the department was viewed as the internal structures, their universities themselves presented a whole range of relationships for the department to negotiate. Then there were the further external alliances and partnership outside their universities that needed to be developed.

In conclusion, if these two universities presidents could reorganize their universities' internal departments operational structure and built clear goals and objectives to let internal departments to know as well as who could change personal attitude and found consultants to assist them to promote their image to let public had more confidence to their universities' education and courses quality. Then, their donations and student enrolment numbers would be caused to increase further possibly.

CHAPTER VIII

Firm producing organization

Helen Reardon is the producer and director of the film, Going North, based on a novel, the best seller list for 16 months and who is considered to be one of the best directors in Hollywood, who already has two Academy Awards to whose credit and many hit motion pictures.Tom Nesson is a promising young actor, his most recent film, the western express was well received on the box office. Because his current popularity, who was chosen to play the leading male part in Going North film.The next days, Tom won't work in about 10 minutes later, who explained that the makeup people were show in getting his makeup on. No one questioned this, any who began where who had staff off yesterday. However, Helen dissatisfied Tom's performance to play his role action during this movie was carrying on.Hence, who had argued. In result, Helen enquired president in the studio executive offices to demand who either dismissed Tom Nesson, actor or dismissed who self. The studio executive did not want to lose either Helen, producer and director of film or Tom actor or both. Neither had a history of being difficult to work with. They were not sure what was causing the problem. This movie seemed to be causing all kinds of problems. e.g. strike and the disagreements between wardrobe and set design. They obviously needed to examine all of the circumstances involved to the making of the film. I supposed to use these communication networks to give reasons why causing problem between Helen and Tom. Communication occurs at several different levels and the communication that occurs among individuals or groups of individuals. This is referred to as interpersonal communication. Networks serve various purposes in organizations and which can used to regulate behaviour, promote innovation, integrate activities and inform and instruct group members. Network also differ in the extent to which who are centralized or decentralized. In centralized networks, all communications pass through a central point or points, so that each member of the network communicates with only a small number of others.Traditional organizational hierarchies, where subordinates communicate to their boss who are centralized networks and all units must communicate with a central headquarter, which then simultaneously coordinates all the units. In decentralized networks, many people or units can communicate with many others.

However, wheel and Y networks are more effective in accomplishing simple tasks and these structures promote efficiency, speed and accuracy by channelling communication through a central person as well as the circle and all channel patterns networks are more effective for complex tasks and communication among all parties facilities the use of group resources to solve complex problems. As this case indicated that Tom won't work in about 10 minutes later, who explained that the makeup people were show in getting his makeup on. No one questioned this, any who began where who had staff off yesterday. Helen and Tom have encountered communication network difficulty. I shall suppose this film producing firm organisational structure is a traditional organizational hierarchies, where subordinates communicate to their department supervisor, e.g. marketing staffs who needed to communicate to marketing manager during who had any problems, then who needed to wait marketing manager to tell to the studio executive president to let him know, so who needed to spend much time to wait studio executive president(central contacting person) to help who to solve problems. Hence, it seemed this movie firm any department staffs who needed spend much time to wait their managers to tell whose problems to studio executive president to know to help them to solve, but who must need to wait whose managers had enough time to help them to deal their problems, then whose conflicts would be solved easily.

The most important influence, the conflicts were between the marketing department and design department and makeup department which would influence Helen, producer and director and Tom, actor whose team co-operation to become more difficult because whether this movie could finish before schedule due date, it must need all departments could cooperate efficiently. Otherwise, any departments' conflicts would influence other teams working performance to be poor in directly, such as Helen, movie of director and Tom, actor whose conflict could be influenced by makeup department and marketing department and design department whose conflicts indirectly. Helen Reardon , the producer and director of the film knew that Tom, film actor went to work in about 10 minutes later next day. However, Helen decided not attempt to enquire makeup department supervisor to explain why the matter had happened directly. Otherwise, who decided to complain Tom's performance to studio executive office directly.I suppose this film producing firm had adapted the wheel and Y networks communication, but these structures are promoted efficiency, speed and accuracy by channelling communication through a central person when the organization structure is simple and there are less staffs work to less departments in its organization. Due to Helen and Tom and studio executive office lacked communication before Tom already did this actor.

So, Helen could not know the makeup department would encounter what kind of problems easily.Due to this film company's organization structure was caused complex , but it still adapted the wheel and Y networks communication structure and these structures are promoted efficiency, speed and accuracy by channelling communication through a central person only. Hence, there were not any makeup staffs could inform to Tom that Helen, film producer and director did not like any staffs worked lately. However, Helen did not meet Tom and the makeup department manager to discuss what actions who demand Tom needed to do to satisfy whose team cooperation together before Tom began to work clearly.Moreover, Helen also dissatisfied Tom's performance to play his role action during this movie was carrying on to cause who had much argument. In result, Helen decided to enquire president in the studio executive offices

to demand who either dismissed Tom Nesson, actor or dismissed who self.Thus, it caused the decision of Helen who enquired the studio executive office president to demand who either dismissed Tom , actor or dismissed who self directly because the studio executive and makeup department manager and Tom, actor and Helen, producer and director of the film between of them lacked effective communication before Tom, actor began to work in first day. If they could spend time to discuss what Tom needed to do to achieve their demand from Helen, producer and director of the film and makeup department, manager before Tom began to do this film. I believe that Tom and Helen problem won't be caused easily.

suggestion of solvable method:

What do you suppose is really causing the problem between Helen and Tom? Explain?

I should recommend this film company needed to adapt the circle or the all channel patterns communication network in its organization. I suppose this film company had many movies to produce at the same time and it was needed more staffs to finish different films in the limited time and it caused the management staffs would not have any time to discuss what kinds of staff problems would encounter in different departments easily.Moreover, it lacked downward communication to low level staffs and studio executive president had not met the makeup department manager and Tom, actor and Helen, producer and director of the film to discuss what their demands were before Tom began to work in the first day. However, studio executive presidents ought communicate to subordinates (actors, producer and director of films, makeup department managers), to provide job instructions, information on organization policies and performance feedback to let them know. Downward communication would be the best way to inform associates about the film company organization's goal and about changes faced by it because this film company had encountered its different departments' conflicts, such as makeup, marketing, design departments as well as staff's individual conflicts, such as Helen, movie director and Tom, actor whose conflicts.

In conclusion, this movie company indicated that Helen, director of the movie complained to studio executive president because who felt dissatisfaction and disagreement Tom, actor' personal behaviour and poor role performance. Hence, this team two staffs who could not build good co-operational relationship to work together to cause whose conflicts in this movie team work because who lacked effective communication before Tom started to work first day.

Discuss the problems between set design and wardrobe and those with the market department.

After few weeks, problems began to arise. Arguments came between the set design staff and wardrobe. They felt that the sets and costumes didn't match. Some thought colours clashed at times. Each group blamed the other, whether whose fault it was. Later, makeup department staffs explained who were being asked to work unreasonable hours. The makeup staff claimed that who had an informal agreement with studio management about the hours they would work and that this agreement had been forced.The problems between set design and wardrobe and those with the market department occurred because they lacked horizontal communication which took place between associates at the same level, e.g. the set design staff and wardrobe staffs felt that the sets and costumes didn't match and some thought colours clashed at times and each group blamed the other, whether whose fault it was. It implied these departments had organizational barriers to communicate effectively to cause these two departments felt difficult cooperation and dissatisfaction and argument occurred, e.g. message/work overload, noise, time pressures, breakdown in the communication network and team cooperation barriers.It also implied these departments had individual barriers to effective communication, e.g. status differences, consideration of self interest, poor listening skills, lacking discussion time etc. In result, it caused conflicts between departments.Later, makeup department staffs explained who were being asked to work unreasonable hours. The makeup staff claimed that who had an informal agreement with studio management about the hours they would work and that this agreement had been forced. This problem occurred that it implied this film company lacked

enough staffs to provide to makeup department to cause who being asked to work unreasonable hours (overtime) and were given unreasonable salary as well as who felt unfair because this movie firm had forced to them to choose to do overtime job forced.

In conclusion, due to design and wardrobe and those with the market department lacked effective communication to discuss whether what furniture design and colour tools to which design department would accept, so it caused market department supplied the design tools to make design department to feel dissatisfactory and it would influence this movie procedure to be late finished finally. Moreover, the makeup department staffs felt unhappily to be enforced to work overtime from management. Some makeup would strike or late to work, who would cause Tom, actor could not have enough time to make up facial and wore dresses to perform during Helen, director of team arrived every time. Thus, some makeup department staffs would strike who should also influence director Helen and actor, Tom whose team cooperation effectively in the beginning.

Could any of the problems in this case have been prevented?

If so? How?

The studio executive offices presidents obviously needed to examine all of the circumstances involved to the making of the film in order to prevent these problems occurred.The first problem referred as below:

Helen Reardon is the producer and director of the film, Going North, based on a novel, the best seller list for 16 months and who is considered to be one of the best directors in Hollywood, who already has two Academy Awards to whose credit and many hit motion pictures.Tom Nesson is a promising young actor, his most recent film, the western express was well received on the box office. Because his current popularity, who was chosen to play the leading male part in Going North film.The next days, Tom won't work in about 10 minutes later, who explained that the makeup people were show in getting his makeup on. No one questioned this, any who began where who had staff off yesterday. However, Helen dissatisfied Tom's performed to play his role action during this movie was carrying on. Hence, who had argued. In result, Helen enquired president in the studio executive offices to demand who either dismissed Tom Nesson, actor or dismissed who self.

The studio executive did not want to lose either Helen, producer and director of film as well as Tom both. Neither had a history of being difficult to work with. They were not sure what was causing the problem. This movie seemed to be caused all kinds of problems. e.g. strike and the disagreements was between wardrobe and set design. They obviously needed to examine all of the circumstances involved to the making of the film. Communication must occur at several different levels. On one level is the communication that occurs among individuals or groups of individuals and this is referred to as interpersonal communication.Networks serve various purposes in organizations and staffs need have suitable networks arrangement to integrate activities and inform and instruct group members. Networks also differ in organization extent to which staffs are centralized or decentralized in any organizations. In centralized networks, all

communications pass through a central point or points, so that each member of the network communicates with only a small members.

The problems of this movie firm could be prevented as: Firstly, the personal conflict had been occurred between Tom, actor and Helen , director of this movie, I recommend this film company needed to adapt the circle or the all channel patterns communication network in its organization. I suppose this film company had many movies to produce at the same time and it was needed more effective to finish different films in the short time. Hence, the studio executive office would not have any time to discuss what kind of staff problems would encounter in different departments easily. I also suppose management staffs lacked downward communication to low level staffs, presidents had not met the makeup department manager and Tom, actor and Helen, producer and director of the film to discuss what their demands were before Tom began to work in the first day. However, studio executive presidents ought communicate to subordinates (actors, producer and director of film, makeup department managers) to provide job instructions, information on organization policies and performance feedback let them know. Downward communication is the best way to inform associates about the film company organization's goal and about changes faced by it. The reason is why downward communication is frequently deficient in this regard because this film company had been complained about personal conflict and department conflict during this movie began to produce.If this film company studio executive president who could attempt to enquire whether what Tom and Helen

would encounter any conflicts before Helen decided to accept Tom to do this movie actor, I believe that their team co-operation could work more effectively.Secondly, the two teams' conflict had been occurred between market and design departments, it was due to design department felt that the sets and costumes did not match and colours clashed conflict due to market department did not discuss with design department before market department began to purchase materials.

The problem between set design and wardrobe and those with the market department occurred because they lacked horizontal communication which takes place between associates at the same level, e.g. set design staff and wardrobe staffs would feel that the sets and costumes didn't match and some thought colours clashed at times and each group blamed the other, whether whose fault it is. It implied these departments had organizational barriers to effective communication , which included these problems existed to cause dissatisfaction and argument occurred in these two departments, e.g. work overload, noise, time pressures, breakdown in the communication network and team cooperation barriers.It also implied these departments had individual barriers to effective communication, e.g. status differences, consideration of self interest, lacking decision time, poor listening skills etc.Thus, these marketing department which ought need to contact design department to enquire whether what kinds of furniture design and colour which design department would accept, then their conflict would not influence Tom , actor who started t perform those job at the first day.

Thirdly, the one group conflict had been occurred within makeup department,Later, makeup department staffs explained who were being asked to work unreasonable hours. The makeup

staff claimed that who had an informal agreement with studio management about the hours they would work and that this agreement had been forced. This problem occurred that it implied this film company lacked enough makeup staffs to cause who being asked to work unreasonable hours and unreasonable salary and who felt this firm had been forced to them to choose to do overtime job because the makeup studio management had an informal agreement to demand them to do this overtime job. Finally, they felt makeup department manager refused their demand, so they would decide to complain studio office executive president directly.

If, this movie company's the makeup department manager could spend time to meet this studio executive president directly to discuss how to solve staffs shortage issue before who decided to give overtime to makeup department staffs. It meant that makeup department manager ought not tell whose makeup teams who must need to work overtime for this movie enforcedly. Otherwise, who ought enquire studio executive president's ideas how to solve this staff shortage problem immediately. Then, it would reduce makeup team's conflict due to makeup management could give discussion chance to makeup team and studio executive president both immediately.

How can the problems now be solved?

Due to this film company had communication conflict difficulty. It was without good internal communication within every individual department, e.g. makeup, marketing departments etc. then it was no good external communication between different departments, e.g. design and marketing departments, so it caused personal and group conflicts. In addition, it was possible to image this film company organizational communication could not without conflict because its staffs had different opinions, so their staffs who would not accept other staff's different opinions easily. In fact, this film's organizational communication was necessary for conducting in an effective manner, e.g. studio executive office president needed to spend some time to communicate with makeup department whether what who felt dissatisfaction as well as this movie Tom actor and Helen movie producer and director needed to meet studio executive office president to discuss why their conflict had caused and how their conflict could solve together.Any effective communication is required and is not only for maintaining human relations, but is also for achieving practical experience to show individual or group communications are needed to reduce departments or personal conflicts in this movie firm within organization.However, the makeup department conflict and management team conflict as well as Tom, actor and Helen, director of this movie and studio executive president individual conflict as well as the design and wardrobe department and the market department both group conflict which had those similarities as it was a necessary process, participants (individuals or groups) were actually or apparently influenced by another individual party or group parties and their conflict would influence this movie productive process. In fact, this movie individual or group conflict was a process where it's these staffs deliberately made an effort to prevent efforts of other staffs with an opposing action, which would result in frustrating other department staffs to achieve their goals or satisfied those interests. For example, this movie firm's marketing department horizontal conflicts occurred between employees within the same department, such as marketing manager needed them to work overtime to influence their personal interests due to this movie firm had scared human resource and finance resource in this department. I shall recommend these methods to solve these problems in this movie firm as below:

This film company studio executive presidents can hold different planning meeting with all major parties, e.g. the first parties Tom, actor and Helen, producer and director of this film as well as the second parties makeup department manager and makeup staff represents as well as the third parties, the design and wardrobe department manager and the market department manager. Hence, these department parties can spend some time to discuss their individual and group conflicts about their dissatisfaction and complaint to attempt to give opinions to negotiate in meeting fairly. The film company top management level , studio executive presidents who can enquire these parties' dissatisfaction and complaint directly and who can attempt to give opinions to negotiate these parties to reduce their leaving chance to threaten this film producing process, e.g. design and wardrobe department needs to discuss how to arrange any colour and furniture design to satisfy marketing department needs and executive presidents in their meeting; and the actor, Tom and the producer and director, Helen and executive presidents can spend time to discuss how to solve their conflict in their meeting. This movie firm executive presidents can arrange meeting to discuss with makeup department's staffs how to either increase makeup department staff salaries to let them to accept to do overtime job or it could choose to employ more right numbers staff to reduce makeup department staffs overtime or it could adopted makeup department staffs' any opinions in order to reduce their overtime.

In conclusion, of this movie firm management could have downward communication to spend some time to discuss how to solve every teams' conflicts together immediately , I believe that their conflicts would solve immediately.

CHAPTER IX

Nuclear factory organization

Nuclear factory team challenge:

Dan was the supervisor of technical maintenance in the nuclear power facility factory and who had noticed that several of his people were reluctant to follow maintenance procedures. He had been told that the specifications were too complex to understand, that the procedures were often unnecessary,and that the plant engineers did not really appreciate maintenance problems. On the one hand, Dan realized that most of their complaints were just excuses for doing things their own way. On the other hand, Dan did not really know which procedures were important and which were not. That's why

Dan had asked Mary, design engineer to meet with him. Mary, design engineer knew nuclear power plants' procedures are complex and potentially risky and every specification and every procedures had a reason for being there. If Dan, supervisor of technical maintenance ignored one procedure, they might get by with it and nothing happens. But one of them just might do it at the wrong time and it caused serious wrong result in this nuclear power plant. So, Mary needs Dan to explain that they had safety and cost to consider. If they lost expensive equipment how they should lie to pay for it. Dan referred that if they lost a finger or got exposes to much radiation, they would not like that happened either.However, Mary needed Dan to follow her specification and procedures to do, but Dan told Mary this really wasn't what his maintenance staffs wanted and they hoped for a little flexibility and who felt who would not like it, but they would have to do it. Lately that afternoon, Dan decided to met his unit and relayed the instructions and who reminded them of the rules and disciplinary actions for not following procedures. At the end of the meeting, who couldn't decide whether whose decision had done any better than Mary's decision. Harry, technical maintenance staff noticed that he had been assigned the routinely scheduled maintenance on the three feed water pumps. The pumps were normally used only for start up and shutdown and as emergency backup. When the main feed water system malfunctioned, these pumps would activate to keep the steam generator from drying out.

The procedure also specified that the pumps should be serviced and test one at a time and that one pump should be out of service at a time. Harry thought that who needed to take three hours to service the pumps that way, but who could do it in two hours if who shut don together. Finally, who did not follow specification and procedures to do maintenance job from Mary demand and who decided to shorten the normal three time to two hours to finish this pump maintenance service job. This case indicated that the nuclear power plant maintenance job needed Mary, design engineer and Dan, supervisor of technical maintenance to co-operate to give their opinions to make any important decision to follow the specification and procedures to reduce the incident crisis occurrence to cause serious death to workers and damage to nuclear power plants. However, due to Dan who had noticed that several of his people were reluctant to follow maintenance procedures. He had been told that the specifications were too complex to understand, that the procedures were often unnecessary, and that the plant engineers did not really appreciate maintenance problems. In fact, I believe that the bad result would be caused seriously. Hence, Mary needed Dan to discuss this issue urgently. However, Mary needed Dan to follow her specification and procedures to do, but Dan told Mary this really wasn't what his maintenance staffs wanted and they hoped for a little flexibility and who felt who would not like it, but they would have to do it. It implied that Dan still agreed whose technician opinions and refused to accept Mary's opinion to follow specifications and procedure in the maintenance procedure as well as Dan decided to meet whose technicians to notify them the rules and disciplinary actions either who might choose to follow procedures or who might choose not to follow during their maintenance. Hence, it implied Dan gave whose technicians to choose freely and Dan's attitude was not forced to need them to follow easily. I agreed that Dan handled this decision was not the best way.However, it was not right that Dan made decisions to choose of nuclear power plant maintenance job whether technicians ought follow specifications and procedure from Mary or technicians ought not follow specifications and procedure from maintenance units actions in the short time. Because it would increase Dan, supervising maintenance unit technicians death or hurt chance and nuclear power plant damaging change if whose decision was wrong. So, Dan ought need to spend time to discuss and gather information to evaluate whether Mary or technicians' suggestion was more safe and less cost to work in nuclear power plant for long term benefits in their meeting together.

In fact, Dan had not follow the correct steps to make final decision before he accepted whose maintenance units did not need to follow specifications and procedures during who needed to maintain nuclear power plant. The decision making steps include that as defining the maintenance problem, e.g. what maintenance problems were the most important to need technicians followed all specifications and procedures to carry on working; identifying criteria, gathering and evaluating information, e.g. other nuclear power plant maintenance procedure methods; listing and evaluating information; selecting best alternative; implementing and following up and giving feedback to let Mary to know the reason either why who disagreed Mary's suggestion or why who agreed whose maintenance units suggestion or none of final decision was made that Mary and Dan and technicians needed to carry on meeting to discuss clearly. An effective decision was as one that was timely, that was acceptable to those affected by it, and

that satisfied the key decision criteria, and it was in the systematic and logical process. Mary and Dan and maintenance units had not ever sat down to discuss this issue in any once meeting together. Dan only met Mary and Dan only met maintenance units individual to discuss this issue separately.He did not give chance to let them to discuss with him in meeting room by face to face contact. Hence, they could not have complete knowledge about all possible alternatives to achieve their potential results effectively because who lacked enough time to make decision making and one good decision making needs a cognitive activity that relies on both perception and judgement. If two people used different approaches to solve problem in the processes of perception and judgement, they were likely to make quite different decision, even if the facts and objectives are identical. As Mary and Dan used different approaches to solve maintenance procedure problem in the process of perception and judgement to decide decision whether the maintenance units needed to follow specifications and procedure or they did not need to follow during technicians did maintenance job in nuclear power plant. Thus, Dan could not ensure technicians' decision whether which was better than Mary's decision because who lacked complete knowledge about all possible alternatives to make final decision before. In conclusion, Dan ought spend time to follow correct decision steps to make decision and who also needed to give them to discuss this issue by face to face contact in meeting and he ought not own objective judgement to agree any one suggestion, who ought give them to make subjective judgement to discuss to accept whose decision freely.

Hence, Dan ought to be one participant role and ought not be one controller role in this decision making procedure.

suggestion of solvable method:

Analyze the critical problem in Part A of the case.

Did Dan handle it in the best way?

What decision styles did he use?

Decisions are reflected the person's preference for one of two perceptual styles and one of two judgement styles. Dan seemed to use intuition style decision, who disliked details and time required to sort and interpret them and whose decision made using this style was based on imagination and Dan believed that whose creativity could help Mary and technicians both to choose whose decision was more suitable. For example, Dan did not spend time to follow decision steps to make decision and Dan did not let Mary and maintenance units and him had chance to meet to discuss this issue by face to face contact to decide whether whose decision was less risky and logical to maintenance units work in nuclear power plant easily. Dan was also a feeling style person to make whose judgement. A feeling style meant a decision style focused on subjective evaluation and the emotional reactions of others. Dan preferred to rely on whose emotions and personal subjective judgements to agree maintenance units' decision. At the earlier, Dan had noticed that several of his people were reluctant to follow maintenance procedures. He had been told that the specifications were too complex to understand, that the procedures were often unnecessary, and that the plant engineers did not really appreciate maintenance problems. So, Dan had accepted maintenance units' suggestion to make judge and Dan had not think and analysed their suggestion clearly. So, Dan chose maintenance units decision was based their feeling and emotion reactions. Before,Dan was met to enquire whose suggestion from Mary. Dan would not accept her suggestion easily, even Mary let Dan to know what the serious crisis would have more chance to occur if his maintenance units did not follow specifications and procedure during they were carrying on maintaining job. However, Dan had not change to accept maintenance units' suggestion easily due to they had influenced Dan's feeling and emotion to judge this issue early.

In what important ways is Harry's behaviour different from Marv's?

During the nuclear power facilities occurred problem, Mary and Harry's both behaviour performance could be seemed as these four aspects to evaluate, such as judgement effort and decision making effort and crisis management effort and time management effort aspects.The important ways is Harry's behaviour different from Marv's included as below: Marv Bradbury, technician was working shift time in nuclear power facility plant. In fact, most technicians did not like this shift, but Marv discovered that who enjoyed this job after few months and who also liked sleep in the mornings and many of this co-workers complained his behaviour to influence poor team work. Marv's job in the nuclear power plant was particular important. Marv's primary was to monitor a series of dials

and readouts in the control room. In fact, the system was so automatic, so who did not spend much time to do this duty of control and manage this system. However, if the readings indicated some variance in the system whose responsibilities were great, who would needed to do duty of interpret the readings, diagnose the problem as well as who would needed to do initiate corrective actions if the automatic correcting system failed. For two reasons, Marv never worried about his responsibilities because the system was fault free and self correcting and it was a good system with no weaknesses as well as Marv had confidence to understand about the system and he was trained always knew what he had to do in the event of a problem and was capable of doing it. In fact, the system occurred problem and who attempted to solve, but who felt difficult to deal. Hence, Marv felt the system was in serve trouble and decided to phone to get help. Although, who could not solve this system problem, but who knew the result if the systems dried out, the temperature was really going to go up and that the core was going to be damaged. Hence, the nuclear power facilities would cause to damaged. However, it took minutes to get someone to attempt to solve this system trouble, but it was too late and no one seemed to know what to do.

On judgement effort and decision making effort aspects, Marv's behaviour performance was seemed as team co-operation managed style person. On the one hand, who lacked decision making effort and who could not attempt to solve problem himself and who needed team co-operation to work together to increase confidence to solve problem. On the other hand, who lacked judgement effort to know whether what who ought need to attempt to solve any during crisis occurred. Moreover, Marv also lacked time management and crisis management efforts.

However, Marv needed to wait eight minutes to get someone to attempt to solve this system trouble, but it was late and no one seemed to know what to do. If the technicians took longer time to arrive, even Marv could not phone to contact them successfully. The result would be more poor seriously. It seemed that Marv could not have confidence to continue to maintain this system. Otherwise, if Marv could attempt to maintain, it was possible that the system could be maintained successfully.

Because Marv felt to make decision making have some degree of risk at this immediate accident occurrence, it would seem that risk taken by a group should be the same as the average risk that would have been taken by the individual group members acting alone (himself). Hence, who decided not to do action

to attempt to solve this trouble, who decided to phone other technician team members to wait their arrival after eight minutes to attempt to solve this trouble, but it was too late and no one seemed to know what to do. However, if who could attempt to solve this trouble within eight minutes, it is possible that this trouble would solve from himself alone.

Harry, technical maintenance staff noticed that he had been assigned the routinely scheduled maintenance on the three feed water pumps. The pumps were normally used only for start up and shutdown and as emergency backup. When the main feed water system malfunctioned, these pumps would activate to

keep the steam generator from drying out. The procedure also specified that the pumps should be serviced and test one at a time and that one pump should be out of service at a time.

Harry thought that who needed to take three hours to service the pumps that way, but who could do it in two hours if who shut don together. Finally, who did not follow specification and procedures to do maintenance job from Mary demand and who decided to shorten the normal three time to two hours to

finish this pump maintenance service job. Two hours later he was done and he packed up his tools and hurried to get home.

On crisis management and time management effort aspects, Harry's behaviour performance was seemed as self managed style. He could attempt to accept risk to decide how to solve problem from himself effort and who had effort to judge how to deal in any crisis occurrence and time management. Hence, it could prove who could deal any crisis occurrence alone and who did not spend time to wait any team members (technician group) assistance, although who could not ensure whose decision whether it was right or wrong. Hence, it implied who

was one confident person.Harry, technical maintenance staff noticed that

he had been assigned the routinely scheduled maintenance on the three feed water pumps. The pumps were normally used only for start up and shutdown and as emergency
backup. When the main feed water system malfunctioned, these pumps would activate to keep the steam generator from drying out. The procedure also specified that the pumps should be serviced and test one at a time and that one pump should be out of service at a time. Harry thought that who needed to take three hours to service the pumps that way, but who could do it in two hours if who shut don together. Finally, who did not follow specification and procedures to do maintenance job from Mary demand and who decided to shorten the normal three time to two hours to finish this pump maintenance service job. Two hours later he was done and he packed up his tools and hurried to get home. On judgement and decision making effort aspects, Harry's behaviour performed who can attempt to judge what action was possible more right to solve this trouble, although who could not ensure whose action is right or wrong, who could make decision to attempt to finish whose job and who felt who would not need to spend time to wait other team members (technicians) to make any decision to work together. Hence, who performed that who was one confident person. In conclusion, risk exist when the outcome of a chosen course of action is not certain. Most decisions in business carry some degree of risk. In choosing between less and more risky options, an individual's risk taking propensity, or willingness to take chances, often plays a role. Two persons with different propensities to take risks may make different decisions when confronted with identical decision situations and information. One who is willing to face the possibility if loss, for example, may select a riskier alternative, whereas another person will choose for taking risks. As Harry and Marv who were working in this same nuclear power facility plant, when the crisis occurred, whose performance would have different to decide to cause different result. Due to Harry performed behaviour was more confident and more judgement effort and self managed person who could accept risk to attempt to make decision alone and disregarded whether the result was right or wrong . Otherwise, Marv performed behaviour was lacked confidence and less judgement effort and team managed person who could not accept risk to attempt to make decision alone and regarded whether the result was right absolutely. Hence, their performance caused the result was also different, as Harry decided to spend two hours to solve the system trouble alone. Although Marv was not sure that Harry's action

whether was correct or incorrect and it needed time to wait whether the system would occur trouble again or not. However, Harry had

attempted to finish whose duties. Otherwise, Marv decided to phone to ask technicians to assist whom and they arrived after eight minutes and who attempted to co-operate to work together. But it was too late and no anyone seemed to know what to do and the system trouble would not still be solve. Hence, it was ensure that the system must be existed trouble and Marv decided not to continue to solve this problem individually and it seemed that Marv could not finish whose duties definitely. Otherwise, Harry could attempt to solve this system trouble alone although it needed time to wait. It seemed that Harry, technician had more strategic decision ability and performed better to compare Marv to deal any crisis occurrence in the nuclear power plant and it seemed that who could assist Dan, supervisor technical maintenance in whose team effectively, although the system needed time to wait to confirm whether it was needed to maintain or needed not maintain again after Macv spent two hours to attempt to maintain. However, it seemed that Harry had more judgement and decision making and crisis management and time management efforts to compare Marv to do this technician position in this nuclear power plant.

How might group decision making be applied at the end of Part B?

The group decision making might be applied to Marv, technician shift team as below:

In general ,in high involvement organizations, associates participate in many decisions with lower level and middle level managers and where low level and middle level managers participate in decisions with senior level managers as well as teams of associates can also make some decisions without managerial input. In this way, human capital throughout the organization is utilized effectively. However, group decision making is similar in some ways to individual decision making because the purpose of group decision makes to arrive a preferred solution to a problem, the group must use the same

basic decision making steps: such as defining problem, identifying criteria, gathering and evaluating information, listing and evaluating alternative, choosing the best alternatives and implementing it finally. Groups are made up of multiple individual, however, resulting in dynamic and interpersonal processes that make group decision making different from decision making by individual. For instance, some members of the decision group will arrive with their own expectation, problem definition and predetermined solutions. These characteristics are likely to cause some interpersonal problems among group members. Also some members will have given more thought to the decision situation than other members' expectation about what is to be accomplished may differ. Thus, a group leader may be more concerned with a collection of individuals into a collaborative decision making team than with the development of individual decision making skills.

In fact, group processes that occur during decision making often prevent full decision of facts and alternatives. Group norms, member roles, dysfunctional communication pattern, and too much cohesiveness may deter the group to produce ineffective decisions. Marv Bradbury, technician was working shift time in nuclear power facility plant. In fact, most technicians did not like this shift, but Marv discovered that who enjoyed this job after few months and who also liked sleep in the mornings and many of this co-workers complained his behaviour to influence poor team work. Marv's job in the nuclear power plant was particular important. His primary was to monitor a series of dials and readouts in the control room. In fact, the system was so automatic, so who did not spend much time to do this duty of control and manage this system. However, if the readings indicated some variance in the system whose responsibilities were great, who would needed to do duty of interpret the readings, diagnose the problem as well as who would need to do initiate corrective actions if the automatic correcting system failed. For two reasons, Marv never worried about his responsibilities because the system was fault free and self correcting and it was s good system with no weaknesses as well as Marv had confidence to understand about the system and he was trained always knew what he had to do in the event of a problem and was capable of doing it. One day, the system occurred problem and who attempted to solve, but who felt difficult to deal. Hence, Marv felt the system was in serve trouble and decided to phone to get help. Although, who could not solve this system problem, but who knew the result if the systems dried out, the temperature was really going to go up and that the core was going to be damaged. Hence, the nuclear power facilities would cause to damaged. However, I felt that it was wrong decision that Marv decided to phone to technicians to wait eight minutes to attempt to find them to solve this system trouble, but it was too late and no one seemed to know what to do. In the beginning, Marv could attempt to solve this system trouble by individual decision, but then who decided to phone to technician team members to assist who because who wanted to reduce whose action risk alone. After eight minutes, these technician team members arrived the nuclear power plant. Marv did not anticipate any actions finally and Marv did not tell technicians how to attempt to act, so who did not anticipate any group decision among their actions finally. In the result, these technicians group decided to auxiliary pump room and discovered that the three valves were still closed and they decided to open the valves, but it was too late and no one seemed to know what to do. During these technicians group decided to do any actions immediately, their group leader would think to build a positive image (believing this system trouble could solve immediately) under threat (nuclear power facilities

would occur damage possibly). Hence, this technician group leader had already failed possibly and who would decide to attempt to maintain this system together and who decided not to enquire Dan, supervisor of technician to assist them immediately. It was possible that who felt time was not enough to wait supervisor assistance or who could attempt to solve by themselves. Because Marv believed that group think decision making was more successful than individual decision making.

Although, group think did not guarantee a better decision but simply increased that likelihood of such a result. When good judgement and discussion were suppressed, the group decision could be more effective to compare to individual decision, Hence, it was possible that , the group decision making could give some benefits to Marv's individual decision making, which included that group decision making could reduce more errors to than Marv's individual decision alone; group decision making could reduce pressure when technicians gave their opinions to solve this system trouble at the same time; members who could been quiet were assumed to be in complete this job together; they could build complex rationales that effectively discount warnings or information that conflict with their thinking; they could reduce chance to cause them to ignore any dangers when they worked at the time and they could discussed any facts, criticisms or evaluations to solve this trouble together at the short time possibly.Hence, it implied that group making decision still had these benefits to compare to Marv's individual making decision.

What alternatives do you use for reducing the possibility of a similar problem in the future?

In academic decision theory, one fundamental decision rule is that of maximizing expected utility. This is the idea that when company

management needs to make a decision and there are different choices, each choice has a set of possible outcome with different probabilities. The problem with this procedures
is that in real life the probabilities and utilities are often different to determine. Of course, if the outcomes are more or less certain. There might be more than one item you like and you might have a hard time to choose just one, but choose any one of choice will be a rational choice. More generally, what we should be when we make decisions is to list the pros and cons of each option available to use (the reasons supporting the option and the reasons against it). Management then choose the option that on balance has the most reasons in its favour. A good decision process requires all time parts being implemented correctly. For example, Is it clear what we have to decide? What is the most important or urgent decision? Are all the options realistic? Are there other options we should consider? Are we overlooked any good or bad consequences of an option? Is there any special criteria for the decision, we should be aware of?

Have the criteria been applied wrongly?

Main reasons why people are failure in their creative idea because failure due to lack of part knowledge and relevant skills and failure of concept and wrong with the initial idea or theory and failure of judgement due to management can have the right idea, but make the wrong decision in executing and developing it and due to failure of attitude and forging a new path where others have not gone before requires courage and the right balance of attitude and due to fear to failure to cause management to abandon an idea before it comes to success.
I recommend that Harry, engineer and Dan, supervisor and Dan's group of normal shift and part time technicians who needed have group discussion to decide what were the serious or common problems as well as whether these system problems which needed to follow specification and procedures
or which needed not to follow specification and procedures during who needed to carry on working daily in this nuclear power plant. Because who should not have enough time to predict or evaluate to judge whether which system troubles issues were serious and which system troubles issues were common to decide whether which needed to follow specification and procedures to carry on maintaining job.
Thus, this decision ought be more fair between Harry and technicians to reduce their conflicts. However, in this situation, group decision making (Harry, engineer and Dan, supervisor of maintenance groups and technicians

discussion together) must be better than individual decision making (Harry, engineer and

Dan, supervisor of maintenance group discussion together).

The group decision making advantage is better quality, or least a significant chance of better quality, particularly when complex decisions are being made. The advantage is based on the fact that groups bring more knowledge and facts to make decision and engage in a richer assessment of alternatives. Other advantages include making better of decisions and greater satisfaction in the organization and personal growth for group members. However, time is one several disadvantages associated with using a group to make a decision. Thus, if they had already discussed this issue to make group decision making before any system troubles existed trouble . Then, these technicians would know whether which system troubles were more serious and which system troubles were common to judge whether either which system troubles needed to follow specification and procedures or which system troubles did not need to follow specification. For example, as the shift time technician, Marv and another full time technician who could not judge whether system troubles were serious or not, so who should felt doubt and difficult whether who ought follow all instruction to finish system maintained work or who ought not follow al instruction to finish system maintained work.

Even, Marv decided to phone to technicians to ask their help. Marv would cause these technicians felt difficult to make group think to make decision in the short time. Group think is a more extreme problem where the pressure to conform hinders critical analysis and creativity, resulting in poor decision making, it might include outsiders who disagree and morality superior. These members are likely to feel more comfortable with each other, but who might also mistakenly perceive themselves as creative. In conclusion, group decision making ought be needed between Harry, engineer and Dan, supervisor of maintenance and technicians before other new system troubles occurred.

CHAPTER X

Electronic assemblies factory organization

Electronic assemblies factory workers team performance

The best ways evaluate to measure what factors are seemed to be influencing this company electronic assemblies products manufactory factory workers team performance.

Firstly, we need to know what kind of methods which can be used to measure team performance, then, we can follow these measurement methods to judge what factors are seemed to be influencing this team performance more actually. Effectiveness and efficiency are the best ways to evaluate team performance. Efficiency is oriented towards successful input transformation into outputs. Effectiveness measures how outputs interact with the economic and social environment and it is being used to reflect overall performance of the team. This company electronic assemblies products manufactory factory team of workers could be evaluated team performance in terms of effectiveness. It's main focus is to achieve team's mission, goals and vision, such as whether how many workers could attempt to finish to wire eight assemblies an hour to meet their one client, Pacific electronic company to know how many assemblies of numbers had been finished to wire currently in order to meet whose Pacific electronic company client shipping schedule or not. At the same time, which value these electronic assembly workers whose performance in terms of their efficiency which relates to the optimal use of resources to achieve the desired output, such as whether how many worker numbers and machine tool numbers would be needed to provide to wire assembly numbers to finish in order to meet whose Pacific electronic company client shipping schedule or not. However, this team performance would have this question ,such as whether there was a difference if this team was effective yet inefficient. Hence, this team would face unprecedented

challenges (factors) which were seemed to be influencing team performance. The first factor was such as, it's client Pacific electronic company needed shorten time to finish wire assemblies which was the main factor to influence performance, such as this team workers would feel difficult to increase to wire eight assemblies an hour from three assemblies an hour, so who would feel anxiety to meet the shipping schedule to finish whose job and quality of assemblies production could not be satisfied to Pacific electronic company client possibly.

The second factor was such as, this company factory and office team management structural relationship. Usually, high team performance has strong upper management and human resource

standards which had been set in place. Because of high team performance expectation, right staffs were being hired to fulfil the positions in order to employees were well aware of the performance measurement and the importance achieve the excellence in their duties. Due to a high degree level of employee involvement needed to be in the team production process, the entity was awarded with staffs commitment which reduced rotation level and the cost associated with the hiring and training process. Hence, employees who were devoted to the team were well aware of necessary knowledge and skill and experience to create unique solutions for clients. Training can be an essential tool for maintaining and improving the productivity of staffs and relevance of skill. The ongoing shortages of labour and skill, the company should be taking

action to reduce the impact of staffs scarcity by training staffs who already had employed. Development opportunities were provided to motivate staffs by providing them with skill and

knowledge enrichment . At the same time, a better skilled, more motivated workforce would help boost competitiveness, improved productivity and increased profit margin.

Moreover, this company lacked good team communication relationship, such as Bill, factory team supervisor who only knew whose same workers of team, such as some of workers Dennis and Steve and Jack who would feel difficult because whose workers were supposed to wire three assemblies

an hour normally with five years, but who were supposed to do eight assemblies an hour to sudden meet one client, Pacific electronic company client schedule to finish confidently as well as who would feel dissatisfactory, due to whose wages did not increase much more to pay for performance to the optimal compensation currently and these workers lacked enough training to face this sudden change to face this client's demand. Thus, it was possible that to influence whose team performance to be poor due to who could not adapt this sudden change from this client's demand. Due to Bill, electronic factory supervisor had not communicate to face to face to contact to enquire whose workers whether what reasons to cause who would feel difficulties if who needed to increase to finish wire assemblies and attempted to find solved methods due to sudden clients' demand. Hence, Bill could not have knowledge and skill to judge whether the reasons were either the numbers of workers or machines were not enough or both to cause that they would

feel difficulties to increase their speed and effort to finish up to eight wire assemblies of numbers to meet this clients' current schedule sudden change demand at this moment.

The third factor was whether this company had effective strategic approaches to this team. A high team performance which maintains five major approaches: They include strategy, customers, leadership, processes and structure , values and beliefs. Strategic approach takes the team to a higher plan of maturity with a vision where the entity is going; customer approach strives for loyalty; leadership approach is associated with management knowledge to transfer the strategy

to employees (teams) level and which will have a direct impact on their behaviour and beliefs and teams' processes and structure and high performance team will strive for implementing innovative policies to support team strategy; the last model is value and belief which translates into team ability to implement the strategy. In fact, this team lacked effective strategic approaches, such as Mr Martin, office manager did not told Bill, electronic factory team supervisor how to lead whose team to a higher plan to maturity with a vision where the entity was going, such as team lacked training or team lacked enough numbers of worker and machine to provide to increase to produce up to eight wire assemblies of numbers to meet this client's schedule shorten change demand to cause this team lacked evaluation to measure every worker individual effort to judge whether who ought have effort to already to finish more wire assemblies of numbers and who ought increase their wages due to they had more effort to raise more productivity to produce eight assemblies or more numbers. Hence, it caused the effort workers did not like to increase the productivity to meet this client sudden change easily due to who felt unfair treatment to compare the other less effort workers in this team. However, the Pacific electronic company client would lose confidence

to Mr Martin office manager if who could not accept Dave, shop of supervisor suggestion either to add some more incentive bonus to these workers to raise whose productivity or providing training or providing more machine and worker numbers to attempt to assist current workers ability to meet the client's schedule. Otherwise, it would cause this client did not choose to find its help next time again. The important factor was whether this factory supervisor and shop supervisor and office manager who had effective communication to predict how to solve any sudden clients' order change trouble between of them. However, I think that, Bill factory supervisor lacked effective leadership to whose workers team in this factory, such as it seemed that some workers; Dennis, Steve and Jack who responded to Bill factory supervisor who felt difficulties to wire eight assemblies an hour suddenly. In fact, some of them had confidence to finish who told lie to Bill because Bill, factory supervisor could not be a good leader to know how to lead whose team to wire assemblies efficiently and effectively daily. Thus, Bill's leadership would have a direct impact on team workers behaviour and team performance poorly if Bill could not change whose leadership skill and who needed to facilitate workers team performance rather than to direct the team, due to who was a formal leader to their team. The company lacked value and belief with translated into team ability to implement the strategy, such as Mr Martin, office manager could not communicate with Dave, shop of supervisor and Bill, factory of supervisor by face to face contact to discuss whether how who could raise to produce wire assemblies of numbers during any clients' sudden shorten schedule occurrence before, so it caused this factory workers team had not more confident to increase to

produce more eight wire assemblies of numbers one hour due to this clients' schedule sudden shorten change. Otherwise, if who could often to discuss to suggest any methods to raise these factory team productivity, this factory leader, Bill would have enough time to plan already how to lead whose factory team workers to co-operate to raise productivity efficiency and effectively in this shorten schedule.

suggestion eolvable method:

Identify the team norms and goals. Are they compatible with organizational objective?

What factors seem to be influencing team performance?

I felt that some of this electronic company factory team norms and goals are compatible with organizational objectives in some situations, but some of whose team norms and goals are not compatible with organizational objective in some situation. Norms mean rules or standards that regulate the team's behaviour and providing direction and are part of the team's mental model. When individual team members violate team norms, some type of punishment is usually applied. Although, norms allow teams be function smoothly, who can sometimes be harmful to team members. It is important that teams develop norms that both foster team productivity and performance and promote the welfare of individual members. This company goal was that it's factory team needed to finish identified wire assemblies of numbers to satisfy every business clients to meet whose identified schedules individually. Hence, Bill, the electronic factory team supervisor who needed to follow Dave, shop of supervisor's instruction to inform whose workers team to finish all wire assemblies of numbers to meet every business client's identified schedule on or before due date. Thus, Bill , factory team supervisor needed to give team norms to let whose team of workers to know whose factory's rules or standards that regulated whose workers teams individually behaviour and providing direction to let them to know when (what the client schedule date was) and what the wire assemblies of numbers the team which must need to finish to deliver to whose clients by shipping. Hence, this factory's rules and standards regulation could be one part to this factory team's mental models on this aspect to achieve this factory workers team norms were compatible with this organizational objective.

Although, the factory workers team norms allowed them to function smoothly, but Bill, factory supervisor could sometimes be harmful to the factory workers team to influence whether

the factory workers team productivity and performance standards level of those wire assemblies of products quality, such as Bill, factory supervisor informed to those factory workers team to increase to produce eight wire assemblies of numbers one hour for normal three wire assemblies of numbers one hour suddenly. It was caused these workers felt anxious whether who should be dismissed if who could not attempt to produce eight wire assemblies of numbers one hour from Bill, factory supervisor demand. It seemed that the factory workers team norms and goals were not compatible with this company

organizational objectives because this company organizational objective was needed workers finished to produce three wire assemblies of numbers to deliver to every client before schedule

due date. It was depended on the situation of the factory whether it had enough time and machine and skilful worker numbers to supply to finish the identified wire assemblies of numbers to every client identified schedule individually. Otherwise, currently, on this situation, it seemed that this factory lacked enough worker and machine numbers and enough time and training to those old(current workers), it caused who felt difficult that every worker needed to finish to produce eight wire eight assemblies of numbers minimum per hour to meet this Pacific electronic company client's identified schedule change suddenly. It also seemed that this company current organizational objective was not same to its prior (past)

organizational objective, such as every team worker needed to finish to produce three wire assemblies of numbers minimum per hour before to meet this Pacific electronic company client's

identified schedule change suddenly. It was given more difficult to let this factory team every worker to attempt to finish to produce eight wire assemblies of numbers minimum per hour

to meet this current Pacific electronic company client's sudden schedule change. Hence, in this situation, I should feel this factory team norms and goals were not compatible with their company's past organizational objective for this Pacific electronic company's earliest past three wire assemblies of numbers of every worker individual production demand

in the identified schedule. In this situation, this Pacific electronic company client's wire assemblies of production numbers needed to be changed which caused this company factory team expectation schedule and wire assemblies

of production numbers, such as every worker needed to produce eight wire assemblies minimum per hour of numbers of it's production goals and should be changed, but this factory team norms and production goals was still same to this Pacific electronic company client's earliest production numbers, such as every worker needed to produce three wire assemblies of numbers per hour. It meant that who needed have more time and worker and machine numbers to assist them to finish to produce if some workers had no enough effort to produce eight assemblies of numbers per hour to finish to meet this client's identified schedule change, otherwise, who needed to extend time to finish this client's production numbers schedule if none of them could produce eight wire assemblies of numbers at minimum one hour. This, this factory team norms and goals

seemed that who were not compatible with organizational client's current objective to every worker needed to increase to produce eight wire assemblies of numbers per hour to finish to meet this Pacific electronic company client prior (not changed) schedule possible. Otherwise, these current factory workers could increase to finish eight wire assemblies of numbers to meet this client's current schedule goals. If this factory team some workers could finish eight or even more wire assemblies of numbers of numbers per hour individually. Thus, this team productivity could still achieve this client's expectation goals to finish to meet on or before schedule. It implied that this team norms and goals was compatible with organizational current objective due to client's expectation wire assemblies of overall increasing numbers had been finished to meet schedule from this factory team overall productivity together. Thus, it caused why this factory team norms and goals would be compatible with organizational team objective of finishing enough wire assemblies of overall numbers to meet this client's schedule date goals possibly or this factory team norms and goals would not be compatible with organization team objective of not finishing enough wire assemblies of overall numbers to meet this client's schedule date goals possibly.

How does the team function to meet individual needs?

This company, Steve and Jack were electronic wire assemblies products factory manufactory workers (members) among of this factory team, who had worked in this factory team five years. Bill was this company factory supervisor, who needed to supervise this workers team to help every business client to finish every electronic wire assemblies of products order to meet whose identified schedule, then delivered to them by shipping channel. Hence, if Bill, factory supervisor
who could not lead whose workers team to co-operate to produce the identified electronic wire assemblies of products of numbers to finish to meet the individual business client's identified schedule before due date to deliver to them by shipping. It would cause that this company and the
and the client would feel this company Mr Martin, office manager and Dave, shop of supervisor could not achieve their service agreement to finish electronic wire assemblies identifies numbers to deliver to them before schedule due date. The result would cause this company lost this client, even this company would accept guilty from this client's complaint. Hence, Bill, factory supervisor needed to lead whose workers team to work efficiently to achieve whose job responsibility to finish every individual business client identified good quality and non damaged of electronic wire assemblies of products of numbers to deliver to them by shipping before schedule due date.

In fact, this factory workers team was combined (co-operated) by every individual worker. Hence, if Bill, factory supervisor expected whose factory team could have good productivity and efficiency, who must individual needs. Otherwise, if some workers did not like to work hard, who would cause this team to delay to finish the identified electronic wire assemblies of numbers to deliver to the individual business client before the schedule due date. Hence, if ill, factory supervisor could

satisfy every individual worker needs, then Bill could lead this team to perform more effectively and efficiently. If this factory work could be done by individual without any need for teamwork was not necessary in this factory. I supposed that this factory needed different workers worked in different steps to cooperate to finish every electronic wire assembly product. The reason was possible that because the employer felt every worker could be more proficient to practise to finish the identified step to co-operate to work together in one team, thus every worker could be raised productivity and efficiency in team, it could get more benefits than individual worker did all steps to finish every electronic wire assembly product alone in this factory. However, as the number of this factory team workers increased, the need for cooperation also increased. As some point, the effort of Bill, factory supervisor who managed the factory team

who would outweigh the benefit of having more workers and this factory team performance would began to decline. Hence, if this factory team of worker numbers increased suddenly.

Although, every business client's electronic wire assemblies of products individual order finishing time would be reduced possibly, but it seemed that Bill, factory supervisor would

feel more difficult to spend more time to lead this team to manage every individual worker who how to co-operate to work more efficiency and who should also feel difficult to satisfy

individual worker needs if this team increased many worker numbers sudden seriously. Hence, this factory team overall performance of efficiency and effectiveness would begin to decline for long term due to this factory team increased many worker numbers suddenly to cause every individual worker felt that who could not satisfy more needs than before. Team structure means of coordinating formal team efforts. Leaders are appointed and work rules and procedures are detailed and job descriptions specify individual task responsibilities. It is necessary to coordinate the efforts of individuals assigned to the different tasks. Otherwise, tasks may not be performed in the correct sequence and employees may duplicate their efforts or work against each other. It seemed that this factory workers team which electronic wire assembling steps could be similar to bank loan department and collection department steps. If one individual worker who had much effort to finish whose wire assembling job step more quick to compare another less effort worker individual wire assembling job step. It seemed that the much effort worker could have much time to attempt to help the another less effort worker to finish whose step. Hence, it was possible that this factory team function could compare every individual worker's effort whether who could had more effort and time to help other worker to finish whose wire assembly

job step during the less effort worker could not finish whose wire assembling step quickly.Thus, this factory team function could evaluate whether who individual worker had more effort

and much time to attempt to help another less effort individual worker to finish their wire assembling job step for every individual client. It implied that these much effort individual

workers who had needs to pay to optimal compensation more than the less effort individual workers for whose better performance in the factory team. It was possible that the piece pay rate compensation was not suitable to these more effort

individual worker to satisfy whose individual needs to accept in the team because who could increase return to multi tasking, in which the same workers did both easy to observe tasks, such as wire assembling production of every step and hard to observe tasks, such as process improvement of wire assembling production of every step and producing exact wire assembling quantities of output (no more and no less). I suggest this factory ought change piece rate compensation to time rate compensation and gain sharing payment method to the more effort individual worker productivity , the individual more effort worker who could receive time rate compensation plus a usually small amount bonus linked to the productivity of the establishment to this factory team during who could increase

return to multi tasking to assist whom to finish the another job step of less effort worker's wire assembling job duty for any individual client's wire assembling products delivering order before schedule due date. I supposed that this factory team function adopted transfer lines in which individual worker was

transferred between stations either by machines or by a moving conveyor assembly line. In either case, time rates compensation were more advantages than piece rates compensation due to

it was more fair to the every more effort individual worker if who could finish whose wire assembling individual step before schedule due date and who had more time to assist another

less effort worker to help who to finish whose wire assembly step immediately. In result, these every individual workers could raise this team efficiency to help this factory team to finish the identified wire assembly numbers to deliver to any client by shipping before the schedule due date normally. Bill, factory supervisor and Dave shop of supervisor who both could obtain high effort from this factory workers on observable tasks by noticing where the wire assembly inventory piles up between stations, without incurring the costs of piece rates. I supposed that the wire assembling products required operations on different machines, performed in different orders setting up fixed paths for work to travel would have made low effort in

production more observable, but would have made the wire assembling production process very inflexible. Therefore, Bill, factory supervisor needed put each individual worker in charge of a machine that could do several jobs. (each with a negotiated rat) and encouraged this team workers to do each job quickly via piece rates. Since there was recurring demand for each wire assembling product for a long time, management did not have to negotiate new piece rates very often. I suggested that Bill, factory supervisor should design the observable tasks , e.g. the step of wire assembling production to be done by one group of factory workers and the unobservable making improvement to the step of wire assembling production, fixing problems to be done by another group with a different compensation scheme and observable and unobservable tasks were separated in this factory team. Thus, wire assembly production workers focused on producing output and were paid to piece rate. Quality was the responsibility of other departments workers, such as inspectors, who identified defective parts and engineers , who attempted to design less defect wire assembly products and processes, these all individual workers who every was paid time rates. All else equal, the low rates compensation was paid to less effort individual worker per piece and the higher rates and bonus compensation was paid to high effort individual worker per time rate to finish every individual business client's order. Finally, this factory team function could give synergy to achieve an effect of the total output of this factory team is greater than the combined outputs of individual worker working alone.

In conclusion, this factory team function could use time rates and bonus compensation method to pay to the individual more effort every worker to let who to feel this employer was more fair to every individual worker performance. The more effort workers ought have more reasonable compensation to compare the less effort workers in this factory team.

If I was Dave, shop supervisor, what team concepts should I apply? why?

If I was Dave, shop supervisor, I should apply these team concepts to this electronic factory wire assembling team. When, managers assign associates to teams, who often make three common assumptions, which can lead to mistakes; such as, who assume that a large team size always better and who assume that everyone knows how or is suited to work in a team and who assume that people who are similar to each other will work better together and so they can co-operate happily. Group means two or more interdependent individuals who influence one another through social interaction. Thus, if I was Dave, shop supervisor, I and my shop staffs would be one group. Bill,

factory supervisor and factory team workers who would be another group factory workers team ; Mr Martin, office manager and office staffs would be another group top managers team. Our company needed these three groups communicate and co-operate to work together to deliver message between about of us about every individual business client's wire assembly product numbers demand and schedule due date to ensure when every client's order could confirm to finish to deliver to the client by shipping factory supervisor and whose workers was a team

because this team had two or more workers with work roles that required them to be interdependent who operated within a large social system, as our factory performing tasks, such as every individual worker needed to produce every part of wire assembling in different stage relevant to our organization's mission , such as finishing the indicated wire assembling numbers to meet individual client's schedule to deliver to whom by shipping with consequences that affected others inside, such as Bill, factory supervisor and others outside, such as Dave, shop supervisor and Mr Martin , office manager of our organization, such as company and Bill, factory supervisor had membership that was identified to these on factory team and those not on the team, such as Dave, shop supervisor and sellers teams as well as Mr Martin, office manager and office administration teams. Effective team performance can be more difficult to achieve when team members belong to difficult identify groups or when their identification with these groups conflicts with the goals and objectives of the team, such as these factory some workers who felt difficult to raise to produce eight wire assembling from these wire assemblies in this factory team, but Mr Martin, office manager needed Dave, shop supervisor to notify to Bill, factory supervisor to let whose factory workers every one to know whether who could raise productivity to this

eight numbers and who could not, then who decided whether how to solve that Pacific electronic company client could not receive wire assemblies of identified number before schedule due date by shipping. In fact, Dan shop supervisor would had conflict, with Mr Martin, office manager who explained

workers felt wages were less, so who would not worked hard to raise effort to produce more wire assemblies, but Mr Martin , office manager disagreed whose suggestion and who enforced Dan, factory supervisor to enquire whether these factory workers who could do eight wire assemblies possibly, it would cause some workers felt anxious to be dismiss if who could not finish this numbers. This, these group conflicts caused non effective team performance with the factory group goals

and the shop group goals and management group goals which were more different. If I was Dave, shop supervisor of this electronic company, I would apply management team

concept to my shop group because I believed we were both the senior level shop manager and office manager who needed to coordinate the activities of our respective units, e.g. shop top management teams and office top management teams as well as Mr Martin, office management group . Otherwise, Bill, factory supervisor would be production team because workers who needed to supervise whose factory workers group to produce tangible products, such as identified wire assemblies

of numbers to meet every individual client's schedule due date.

A final consideration in Dave, shop supervising team effectiveness is whether a supervising team is needed to perform the work at all or whether the work is best performed by Dave,

shop supervisor individually. I this case, it would have been better to have individual separately, Dave, shop supervising team effectiveness is measured on knowledge criteria, affective criteria and outcome criteria. Knowledge criteria reflected the degree to which Dave, shop supervisor individually increased its performance capability . Affective criteria addressed the question of whether Dave, shop supervisor individually had a fulfilling and satisfying to supervise shop experience, such as whether Dan could manage whose shop and factory effectively. Outcome criteria referred to Dan 's personal quality of the shop supervisor how to supervise whose shop and factory teams effectively. Hence, if I was Dan this electronic company shop supervisor, I shall apply these team concepts to apply to whose shop and factory teams management in this situation.

CHAPTER XI

Brooklyn Bluebirds baseball organization

Brooklyn Bluebirds baseball organization was the best professional team for ten years win competition. A new owner, Trudy Mills, who acquired it to rebuild the team by acquiring big name players intention. However, during the first month end, the team was in the first place with a record of 20 wins and 7 losses, but then conflicts problems began. Conflict is a process in which one party perceives that its interests are being opposed or negatively affected by another party. Firstly, Bluebirds organization encountered the rumors of conflict between players were reported in the sports columns. Russ Thompson, a five years veteran and starting first baseman team player, publicly stated that who wanted to renegotiate his contract. In fact, the reason to Russ, this baseball team player who caused this conflict, due to he was unhappy that whose baseball team current employer, Trudy had brought many baseball players at much higher salaries than him. Hence, it caused Trudy, baseball team player who felt dissatisfactory to whose current employer, he felt who had fire year baseball competitions experiences and who had fire year baseball competitions experiences and who had helped whose baseball team, such as Brooklyn Bluebirds to win much competitions. Hence, who felt Trudy, current Brooklyn Bluebirds baseball owner could not give him higher salaries

than this team's other baseball team players. It was unfair to him. In the result, Russ, baseball team player met with Trudy, Brooklyn Bluebirds baseball team owner and Trudy's lawyer and Bluebird's general baseball team manager to discuss whose salary increasing issue, but the meeting ended in disagreement and both Russ, baseball team player and Trudy, Brooklyn

Bluebirds baseball team owner were angry, it was caused by salary could not increased to Russ, baseball team player disagreement to achieve negotiation conflict within the

Bluebirds organization. It seemed that Russ, baseball team player and Trudy, Bluebirds baseball team employer (owner) whose interpersonal conflict which occurs between their both individuals in this organization. They are personal conflict, it means Trudy, Bluebirds baseball team employer and Russ, baseball team player both conflict that arises out of personal differences between people, such as differing goals, values or personalities, such as the baseball it was possible that Trudy, Bluebirds baseball team owner who would not give high salary to Russ, baseball team player due to who needed to evaluate whose baseball competitions performance with team members to judge whether who ought to increase whose salary, but Russ, baseball team player felt who was unfair to pay him less salary than other baseball players due to who had five years baseball competition experiences. Thus, their differing values were very

different to cause this personal conflict in this Bluebirds baseball team organization. It also seemed that Trudy, baseball team owner existed substantive conflict that involved work content and goals to Russ, baseball player, such as Trudy needed time to evaluate Russ, baseball competitions performance (work content) whether who could help whose baseball team to win competitors (goals) to decide whether who could increase salary. I felt the main factor to cause their personal conflict was that Russ, baseball player felt Trudy, baseball team owner paid him less salary than other baseball players. Instead of this factor, it had also other factors, such as, baseball team organization needed interdependency co-operation specially. Interdependency means work must be coordinated between groups (such as baseball team) or individuals (baseball players). The more interdependent two

groups on individuals are the more the potential for conflict exists. Interdependency can result from limited resources or from required coordination in the timing and sequencing of

activities. Due to Russ, baseball team player needed to co-operate with other baseball team players to attempt to carry on practising to learn how to achieve to win any baseball

competitions intention. Hence, it was possible that Russ would listen rumors of conflict between players who were reported in the baseball players in the baseball sports columns about their salary issue, even it was possible that Russ and other baseball

players who felt Russ and other baseball players who felt difficult to attempt to co-operate to carry on baseball team training within limited time and sequencing of activities before any baseball competitions. It would cause this baseball team group conflict occurrence between baseball team individual players because this baseball team individual players and baseball team group had less control over own team cooperation in this situation.Russ, baseball team player felt who individual abilities were exceed to other baseball team players in this baseball team. In fact, Russ's individual abilities did not sum up to influence this baseball team performance. Russ, individual baseball player skill was only moderately good predictor when two or more team players interacted in a precise way. Due to baseball sport team needed more cooperation and interaction to team every players, so it was necessary the importance of individual ability decreases and groups processed increased.

Hence, the more closer the team players were in their abilities, the more likely who would fully put to use their combined abilities . Thus, it was possible that Russ would feel whose baseball skill and ability was exceed to this team other baseball

players to cause who felt more difficult interdependent to co-operate with the other team baseball players in this baseball team to cause this team difficult co-operational conflict.

Hence, the difficult baseball team cooperation also caused the group conflict due to Russ felt dissatisfactory reward and who felt the other baseball players performance would influence whose performance to be poor to win any further baseball competitions indirectly. Russ, baseball team player was discouraged to leave Trudy, Bluebirds baseball team organization by Marty, baseball team manager indirectly.

Next, Bluebird baseball team organization also encountered conflict between Marty, baseball team manager and Russ and Mickey baseball team players as well as conflict between Marty, baseball team manager and Trudy, baseball team employer (owner) about who planned leaving. Trudy, current baseball employer. This conflict was caused due to Marty, baseball team manager discouraged these two baseball team players both Russ and Mickey continued to serve this employer and encouraged who signed another baseball team employer who could give more salary to them. However, Trudy, this baseball team employer (owner) still felt Russ and Mickey both were the best baseball player and the clients paid to see them player. Hence, Trudy phoned to Marty, baseball team manager to require who to apologize to them and persuaded them did not plan to leave.

Then, Marty baseball team manager made conflict with whose employer, Trudy to indicate himself had been a good baseball team manager to manage whose baseball team players effectively and who felt that who did not need to apologize to Russ and Mickey, these two baseball team players because who had not leave Trudy currently and who had already trained them to play further baseball competitions. This conflict was caused because Marty, baseball team manager who encouraged these two team players to leave due to whose salaries were paid less than other baseball team players. Then, Trudy baseball team employer needed Marty to persuade who did not leave his

baseball organization, but Marty refused to tell them about whose employer instruction. Thus, it caused group substantive conflict due to Russ and Mickey both baseball team players

felt dissatisfaction to work in this baseball team to achieve team cooperation goal with other team players to win any baseball competitions as well as it also caused individual procedural

conflict between Trudy and Marty due to that Trudy, baseball team owner gave responsibilities to Marty, such as Marty, baseball team manager needed to apologize to these two team players and persuaded them did not plan to leave, Marty felt it was not whose responsibilities due to who had finished to manage this baseball team effectively and who ought not need to apologize to them due to who was their manager. However, Trudy felt it was also whose responsibilities. Thus, unreasonable responsibility was a factor to cause Marty felt dissatisfactory to Trudy, baseball team employer to require him to do this apologizing issue.

suggestion of solvable method:

Describe the types of conflict that seem to exist within the Bluebirds organization.

What are the causes?

Is the conflict functional, dysfunctional or both? explain.

Dysfunctional conflict is different to functional conflict as

below:

Dysfunctional conflict is conflict that interferes with performance to organizational goals and objectives, such as doubting about the organization's future performance in the minds of shareholders; conflict can cause people to exercise their own individual power and engage in political behaviour directed toward achieving their own goals; conflict can have negative effects on interpersonal relationships, so it needs to take time and resources and emotional energy to deal with conflict, both on an interpersonal and an organizational level.

Functional conflict is beneficial to organizational goals and objectives . Any organizations without functional conflict frequency lack the energy and ideas to create effective innovation. Conflict can have a number of functional consequences for organizations, such as facilitation of change, improved problem solving or decision making, enhanced morale within a group, more ability in communication and productivity and creativity and stimulation. I felt this Bluebirds baseball team organization had only dysfunctional conflict, such as

Trudy baseball team owner and Marty, baseball team manager who had negative effects on interpersonal relationship. Trudy needed to take time and resources and emotional energy to deal with Marty's individual conflict both on an interpersonal level.

For example, in fact, Marty encouraged Russ and Mickey to leave Trudy's baseball team, but Marty refused to follow Trudy's requirement to apologize to them and persuaded them to stay. It would cause this baseball team other players turnover numbers to be increased due to these two the best baseball players leaving influence and Trudy would lose these two the best baseball performance players finally.

CHAPTER XII

Hill wood Medical Centre organization

Organizational cultures and subcultures will influence Hill wood Medical Centre organizational performance and commitments. The subcultures may take precedence over the organizational culture for individual employees and thus gain their commitment. Hill wood medical centre can therefore focus on the relationships of both organizational culture and subcultures to satisfy staffs need to serve patients in happy work environment. Organizational culture includes leadership style and job satisfactory measurement. Hence, employees' commitment was examined in relation to the level of consent to and conflict with managerial strategy. Although, managerial strategy is not the same as leadership, the attributes and skills required in leadership could be seen as an essential part of

managerial strategy. Organization culture(s) has (have) a causal modelling approach to examine the determinants of organizational commitment and labour turnover. Organization culture(s) can include a variety of variables , e.g. age, pre-employment expectations, perceived job characteristics and the consideration of leadership style, which all influence organizational commitment indirectly via effects on job satisfaction. I supposed that Hill Wood Medical Centre existed relationship of organizational culture and subcultures to influence staffs feel satisfactory and commitment. Also of interest is the relationship of these variables with leadership style, job satisfaction and subject characteristics, such as age, level of education to its staffs in this hospital. In Hill Wood Medical Centre organization, its organizational culture was the

hospital cultures and subcultures which refer to the culture of the wards or work units or operation rooms to every department staff commitments refer to nurses team and medical service chief medical officer team and surgeons team and administrative department etc their different departments' individual staff's commitments. There is a culture relationship between this medical centre organization commitments

and it was measured with administration department and operating rooms and wards department etc different departments' subcultures as well as surgeons and

nurses and doctors and administration staffs etc different teams' subcultures. More specifically, it is expected that such as Hill Wood Medical Centre organizational culture could be more supportive and innovative to its different departments, such as

wards and surgeons operating rooms and administrative office etc different departments subcultures. Thus, I believe there is a strong relationship between this medical centre organizational cultures and subcultures and commitment and characteristics of

this organizational overall culture, such as corporate values and beliefs commitments and performance to Hill Wood Medical Centre organization. However, I think this medical centre's bureaucratic work practices organizational cultures often result in negative employee commitment due to its supportive work

environment could not result in greater commitment and involvement among employees. For example, these different departments needed to met Sharon Lawson, administrator of Hill Wood Medical Centre to discuss how to solve their departments problems in their meetings in that day, but Sharon Lawson could not had any suggestions in these meeting in that day. It seemed that this medical centre had negative culture and subcultures to get negative results due to who needed to spend time to wait Sharon to meet them and the administrator could not give any suggestions to solve their department problems on that day. Such as Holly from state health department told Sharon the general inspection needed to be improved, e.g. kitchen needed cleanliness and inspectors felt this medical centre needed to allow patients access to drug supplies, but this state health department representative had requested inspection before six months and Helen controller asked Sharon about

the new computer hardware who requested six months ago and Helen told Sharon who needed it now for billing efficiency to office use, but Sharon decided to make request to board for computer hardware purchase next meeting and some surgeons were drunk to work in operating rooms, who caused danger to patient's life to cause some patients complained these surgeons, but Sharon did not solve whose complaints at that day immediately and medical staffs were discussing why the medical centre had not purchased one upgraded piece of standard diagnostic equipment used in body scanning $700,000 cost, but Sharon had not enquired whose reasons clearly to decide to buy the equipment next year, but doctors did not understand why Sharon could not purchased this year. Then the nurses agreed to give Sharon a week to investigate the situation and attempted to resolve it and a meeting was scheduled for next week to review the situation. Finally the medical centre's attorney needed to wait for twenty minutes to discuss about what steps were to be taken to solve with surgeons, Dr Chambers who was complained about drunk wine work in surgeon operating rooms issue, but Sharon had no more time to meet whom to discuss on that day. Hence, it seemed that this medical centre had not good culture and subcultures in its organization, such as Sharon had not enough time arrangement to meet them to discuss their departments' problems on the same day. It seemed that Hill Wood Medical Centre had no good

organizational culture and subcultures to cause staffs conflicts and administration department also wasted much time to handle departments' meetings only. If Hill Wood Medical centre culture and subcultures could be changes, such as every department could attempt to discuss how to solve their problems before who met the administrator . Then I believe that who could give reasons or ideas to support their view point to persuade Sharon made final decision to shorten their meeting time. Hence, this medical centre seemed that it's subcultures and culture were negative. I supposed that it's nurses team subcultures tended to identify more cooperation closely with different teams, such as surgeons operating rooms team, doctors team, wards team etc departments to compare the administration department. It meant nurses teams' subcultures needed often exhibit greater loyalty and commitment to these departments in the Hill wood

Medical Centre organization. Thus, it seemed that it needed better subcultures in nurses teams to share different departments' job to reduce staffs conflicts to serve patients satisfactory. However, Hill Wood Medical Centre organizational culture and subcultures could influence

staffs' job satisfaction and commitment positively or negatively due to this medical centre cultural variables could influence their feelings , such as the amount of reward, flexibility of work schedule and balance of work and home life etc. Hence, Hill Wood Medical Centre culture could cause those intrinsic factors to influence every units staffs' feelings of job satisfaction. In relation to educational level and organizational

commitment, it seemed that educational level was negatively relative to this Hill Wood Medical centre, such as it could permit surgeons were drunk to work in operating rooms often, it was danger to every patient life during surgeons were drunk to work . Hill Wood Medical Centre overall culture was from low to top level communication channel and bureaucratic work organizational culture was often in negative employee commitment, such as all departments needed to wait the administrator to arrange meeting time to solve their departments problems in the same day. However, much decisions could not get solutions from the administrator. It seemed that this Hill Wood Medical Centre's bureaucratic organization cultures and subcultures caused Sharon had arranged more meetings on that day to influence who had not enough time to do their departments' duties on that day efficiently due to who only concentrated on handling meetings issues on that day.

I think Sharon Lawson who did not know how to arrange what kinds of job duties and meetings which were more important which ought to handle on that day or what kinds of job duties and meetings which were not more important to handle on the same day. Hence, who could not get any discussion result in these meetings on that day due to Sharon, administrator had not enough time to negotiate their departments to solve problems successfully in meetings. In conclusion, this medical centre organizational cultures and subcultures seemed that which

were not positive to staffs' commitments and job satisfaction. Such as its different departments needed to spend much time to wait administrator to arrange meetings to discuss their problems, but who did not make any decisions in their meetings. The administrator would influence different departments overall work efficiency and effectiveness to be poor. So, it ought need to change its organization culture and subcultures to raise its different departments' efficiency and effectiveness as soon as possible.

suggestion of solvable method:

Describe the culture or cultures at Hill wood Medical Centre ? Are these subcultures ?

How would you recommend that Sharon administrator measure effectiveness at Hill wood Medical Centre?

The medical centre performance effective evaluation meant to measure whether the degree to its overall organization was improving or deteriorating. The measurement combines quantitative and qualitative analysis and efficiency trend to get the degree of effective result. On the quantitative analyses measurement, e.g. medical errors occurrence rates ; patients medical treatment health rates. On the qualitative analysis measurement, e.g.acquiring executives who communicated a culture of quality through personal supportive polities

and investment of resources, such as the degree of diagnostic equipments effectiveness, the degree of staff quality improvement and the degree of health information technological

effectiveness and the degree of every patient's service satisfaction etc. Performance measurement effectiveness is well established throughout medical and health care industry, of which include the core areas of finance, operations, clinical care and information technology services as below:

Finance is an organization often measures the efficiency of its accounts receivable, i.e. timely collection of payment for services rendered, such as this Hill Wood medical centre can collect how much payment for services from patients per week and it earns how much profit or loss per week. Operating is an organization needs the lengths of time to take for a patient to receive an appointment in the practice or measures individual patient whose satisfaction with the care received, such as the satisfactory degree of Hill Wood Medical Centre every patient

how who feel to every doctor, physician, surgeon and nurse whose service performance and personal attitude to whom.

Clinical care is an organization measures how often care is delivered in accordance with evidence based guidelines or how effective that care is in improving every patient outcome,

such as whether Hill Wood medical centre had how many doctor and surgeon and physician and nurse numbers who could treat every patient to be health to satisfy who don't feel sick or

hurt again after who left this hospital. Information technology is an organization widely integrated into health care settings to support for performance measurement, such as whether Hill Wood medical centre needed to buy how many diagnostic equipments to use to body scanning for surgeons or needed to buy how many computers to office to use to achieve the best performance.This Hill Wood medical centre needed these processes to measure its quantified numbers to a health care service provided to on behalf of or by a patient that was needed on scientific evidence of efficiency or effectiveness, so it could quantify a specific system, e.g. getting a test done or a

service performed and it's outcome could measure to quantify every patient's health status resulting from its nurses and doctors and surgeons and physicians whose health care. Thus, in the clinical area, Hill Wood medical centre could measure every patient outcome to compare to every care standard, such as every patient's test value to measure effectiveness. Measurement effectiveness is central to the concept of this Hill Wood medical centre quality improvement, it provides a

mean to define what medical centres or hospitals actually do and to compare that with the original targets in order to identify opportunities for improvement. On clinical care and operational measure aspect:

Hill Wood medical centre ought to establish standardized and systematic procedures for problem solving to able to test and implement major practice changes. Such as clinical

guidelines or care maps for specific conditions or procedures, department specific quality plans with short and long term goals, improved educational and training materials for clinical staff error reduction, hand washing and infection prevention, education materials for patients regarding full prevention, information technology that reduced medication errors and improved data collection etc these changes. To decide whether how much change criteria it ought need to change it's measurement effectiveness was depending on the nature of the

change and the rate of acceptance and adoption of staff. It aimed to resistance to change in culture from surgeons and physicians and nurses and doctors; measured how much limited

resources were available to use or maintain quality related equipment investment, such as office equipments or operational rooms diagnostic equipments of numbers as well as

whether how to make the patient complaint numbers to be reduced to achieve zero tolerance to any staffs as well as whether departmental quality plans could achieve special goals effectiveness measurement as well as whether training could be achieve continuous quality improvement to staffs measure

effectiveness as well as organizational structure change could be raised staffs service performance efficiently, such as whether creation was needed on service quality and addition staff and responsibilities were needed for quality improvement

as well as whether patient care redesign and more training was needed for aides and multi disciplinary leadership teams change. Establishing organizational culture and subcultures of service quality measurement effectiveness aspect as below:

. Setting how long time to achieve short term and long term attainable goals and celebrated successes to individual staff and individual units involved in reaching their goals.

. Keeping the individual unit staff involved in problem identification and problem solving time spending. It aimed to raise everyone to feel much valuing expecting all to participate
to solve any problems in the most shorten time.

On finance and information technology measure effective aspect:

Effective organizational culture and subculture change could encourage every unit leader and peers to be patient, but recognized that changing took time and continuing to keep quality improvement to measure whether it needed how much time to balance quality and financial goals and considering investments, such as how many equipment numbers were needed to buy to provide to office and operational room units to use to raise office productive efficiency and effectiveness as well as operational rooms service efficiency and effectiveness to measure to achieve quality improvement from a short and long term perspective to this Hill Wood medical centre. It aimed to evaluate whether new policies were bringing equipment into
operating rooms or office to use was needed or was not needed .

I recommend Sharon, administrator needed to indicate these qualitative performance effectiveness measurement questions included:

.What barriers did this medical centre face in implementing the strategies or achieving success?

.Did it overcome those obstacles and if so, how?

In conclusion, to measure effectiveness of this medical centre whether how it could achieve quality improvement for success. I recommend Sharon, administrator needed to consider what should be the indicators to include implementation of aggressive quality targets for performance indicators as well as how to decide tightening of recruitment and standards and enhanced respect for all staffs in enhancement of quality improvement processes to shorten time to solve problems in
efficient manner and hoped to decide new investments in quality related information technology combined with the number of staffs input numbers efficiently and effectively.

Thus, the four core areas of performance measurement was one quality improvement models of high performing effective measurement to Hill Wood Medical Centre.

What do you think some of the effectiveness criteria might be?

I think some outcomes of effectiveness criteria to this Hill Wood medical centre, it might be the practice changes appeared to have resulted in

improved outcomes for patients. In
addition to major improvements in the combination quality measures which
based on morality, morbidity and complication rates, such as below:

Process/ operations effectiveness criteria: faster receipt of test result, faster patient flow, easier and more efficient data sharing and recording, fewer medication errors. So, I think it could measure the doctors and nurses and surgeons and physicians who serve to every patient's performance whether what effectiveness criteria to these staffs from their every serving patients' satisfactory level. Health related effectiveness criteria: calculate the reductions in morality rates, e.g. the surgeon reducing numbers were drunk to work in operational rooms every month and the patient health numbers every month.

Work environment and reputation effectiveness criteria: increase in patients satisfaction and staff satisfaction numbers and morale improved status numbers every month in this medical centre. If it could increase the numbers of patients satisfaction and staff satisfaction and morale improved status numbers, it would have greater ability to improve service quality to surgeons and doctors and nurses in this medical centre.

Bottom line effectiveness criteria: the effective measurement of decreasing or increasing costs per medical centre units and length of stay for certain conditions and increased or
decreased patients admission numbers and market share numbers every month. I think it lacked enough equipments for office to use and diagnostic equipments numbers were needed to be upgraded to use in body scanning because the departments leaders needed to met to Sharon, administrator to permit to buy those equipments urgently. It seemed this medical centre service effectiveness criteria would be poor due to there was not enough equipments to provide to these units to use possibly. Hence, if this medical centre could raised the quantitative and qualitative effectiveness criteria as above, it would change positive outcomes to motivate these units doctors, surgeons, nurses, physicians and administrative individual team leaders and their colleagues to strengthen the service quality improvement process to this Hill Wood medical centre. However, I think this Hill Wood medical centre performance was poor from the above
effectiveness criteria analysis. Performance must be defined in relative to explicit goals reflecting the values of various stakeholders. This medical centre internal stakeholders were
such as patients, doctors, nurses, surgeons, physicians etc and external

stakeholders were patients, debtors, banks, Government shareholders etc. This medical centre performance might be defined according to the achievement of specific targets of

either clinic to patient services or internal departmental operations. Targets might relate to traditional hospital functions, such as health treatment, care and rehabilitation as well as administration, ambulatory patient delivered services and health care networks. Following this medical centre evidences which indicated the poor performance of effectiveness criteria, such as Sharon, administrator lacked enough time to meet some department leaders to help them to solve problems successfully on that day, so it caused who needed to make another

meetings to discuss their problems again. It seemed the administrator wasted their time to do other important duties on that day efficiently and effectively. I think Sharon, administrator

was not one effective administrator in this medical centre. If who could not change whose management attitude to co-operate with other department managers(leaders), then who could cause poor subcultures to different departments to build to this medical centre overall organization culture and who also influenced other department performed ineffective and inefficient results due to Sharon, administrator who did not know how to arrange time to meet them everyone efficiently.

In conclusion, I think if this medical centre hoped to reduce doctors and nurses and surgeons and physicians and administrations etc staffs frequently conflict and maximized work effectiveness of its departments. Sharon administrator had responsibility to change whose personal work attitude to adapt their subcultures to co-operate with different departments. Otherwise, this medical centre would not be maximize effectiveness and would increase staffs conflicts to cause staff turnover numbers to be increased seriously.

CHAPTER XIII

KBTZ television organization

KBTZ was a large television station in United States. It was one of the largest revenue producers in its entertainment market and employed more than 180 staffs and it was as the local television

leader in the use of sophisticated electronic equipment.

The station's physical plant was planned to accommodate the new equipment and to boost its image at the leader in the entertainment market. However, its organization development caused much problems to need to solve. On the one hand,

due to external pressure to cause organization change, such as entertainment market competition needed to have high technological new equipments to purchase to provide to different departments to use, e.g. cameras, films etc equipment. Hence, different department staffs needed to learn how to

use these equipments to raise productive performance quality. On the other hand, due to internal pressure to cause organizational change, such as reducing aspiration performance factor was caused poorly in KNTZ organization, which meant gaps was occurred between what an individual, unit or organization wanted to achieve and what it was actually achieving in KTZ organization. Due to KBTZ television station's operational department ,engineering department, programming department, sales department, news department etc departments which every department individual staff, work group, division or overall KBTZ organization was not meeting its own expectations to adopt KBTZ new organization changes as well as television programming needed new productive tactics to change new strategies and processes often caused follow poor performing individual staffs, units and KBTZ whole organization, which might reduce aspiration levels instead of making changes sufficient to increase performance. Because KBTZ large television station often compared itself with other

television stations in the entertainment industry , when comparisons with similar others suggested that better performance was possible. However, KBTZ staffs could not adopt organizational change development suddenly, so it caused many different departments felt difficult co-operation together in KBTZ television station organization. In fact, American television station entertainment industry was encountered by life cycle forces, it meant the natural and predictable pressures that built as to KBTZ television station organization grew and that KBTZ television station must hope to continue growing.

Hence, KBTZ television station was at elaboration stage, it meant KBTZ needed for balance, focused on efficiency and innovation, formal procedures existed and empowered low level

managers and associates in its organization if KBTZ still wanted to keep its large television station position in United States. However, KBTZ 's large television station's physical plant planned to accommodate the new advances equipment to provide different departments staffs to use and to boost its image as the leader in the United States entertainment market. It would cause its staffs feel difficult to adapt to adjust efficient and effective co-operation between departments due to it's planning change caused a process involving deliberate efforts to move KBTZ television station within its organization undesirable state to a new and more desirable state during KBTZ 's organization development was carrying on. Hence, due to its organization development change it would cause these basic problems at KBTZ organization as below:

suggestion of solvable method:

As I was the KBTZ consultant to meet with Valerie Diaz, president and general manager, who explained the key problem as:

The first problem was the high stress to which KBTZ 's manager and associates who felt about time deadlines in television problem, e.g. when it's precisely six o'clock , KBTZ news department staffs must be on the air with the news. All of the news material, local reporting, news, interviews must be processed, edited and ready to go at six o'clock. This news department staffs felt difficult, due to who could not have any half prepared material extended deadlines to cause lose the KBTZ 's audiences. This situation caused a great deal of

conflict and turnover increased, such as a number of well qualified and motivated employees were leaving KBTZ television station. The news department's employee turnover was about 35% which was too high as well as KBTZ also had trouble hiring qualified people who fit their culture and these new qualified staffs feel difficult to co-operate with KBTZ staffs to cause conflict. It seemed to be team conflict problem.

The second problem was that business manager felt difficult to manage different departments, due to who previously worked in sales and in the general manager's office, but who lacked management training and this was whose first managerial position to help in managing whose departments.
It seemed to be personal difficult management problem.

The third problem seemed the news department and business office and programming department indicated who felt the new director who lacked leadership ability to manage any

departments, such as new department managers and associates felt extreme dissatisfaction with the department head, new director who had very negative attitudes toward their overall

work environment , new director lacked leadership ability to let news department managers and associates communicate easily. Moreover, news department associates also complained of very

low reward, including pay, promotion opportunities and managerial praise and who also complained of constant criticism, which was the only form of managerial feedback onperformance. Hence, it implied the new director did not attempt to solve any departments staffs

difficulties to adopt new organization change to cause their dissatisfaction and conflict and complaints occurrence to whom. It seemed to be new director personal leadership problem and

news departments staffs team communication and individual dissatisfaction problems.

The fourth problem was operations department manager who complained another departments, such as news department staffs, who were confused all of the time and engineering groups, staffs were lazy and who did like cooperation to influence operational department performed ineffectively, due to these groups needed to co-operate to work together. So operations manager suggested me (KBTZ 's consultant) dismissed chief engineer and shaped up (reorganized) the news groups and the engineers groups . It seemed to be difficult co-operation occurred between operations department and engineering and news both departments problem.

The fifth problem was chief engineers who complained the unreasonableness of certain people in other departments. For example, the difficulty indicated that whose team engineers could not immediately repair some malfunctioning equipment in their area and it could take several hours just to determine the cause of the failure. It seemed that engineer department lacked enough engineers and equipments were provided to them to work from operational department . It caused team conflict problem.

The sixth problem was the program director complained the station was missing a lot of opportunities in other areas, e.g. news and sales, the chief engineer was incompetent and operations managers were difficult to motivate low level managers to make any decisions or took any responsibilities . It seemed the program director who felt dissatisfactory to other

departments personal performance problem.

The seventh problem was the promotion manger who expected a little training to provide in how to deal with people, innovation and communication problems. It seemed that promotion manager felt difficult to adopt new organization change problem.

The eighth problem was sales department representatives complained who ought to increase salaries due to whose good sale performance. It seemed that sales representatives'

dissatisfactory problem. Finally, the business office and programming department also made one survey to indicate

individuals in these departments to have generally positive attitude, such as job satisfaction, but who had two important negative attitude in whose working environment.In general, these low and middle level staffs whose negative attitude of task environment major problem indicated who thought that whose department heads and the general manager could handle downward communication better , it meant that the middle and low level staffs felt the top level managers lacked effective communication to them as well as these were several comments about being underpaid relative to other station employees.

Although, the survey indicated the managers and associates whose high satisfaction, but who also believed that the negative factors led them to be poorly motivated. Such as some low and middle level associates reported that who were not sure who was

top level immediate manager , since both the assignments editor and the assistant news director gave them assignments. It seemed that who lacked communication between departments to

influence who did not know who had actual authority to give job to them to do. It would cause difficult to co-operation to finish every job between department. If the assignments

needed to finish urgently, who would influence any news, entertainment programmes could not been finished before the time deadlines. It seemed to be team communication problem.

The another problem was that, some low and middle level associates also reported that creativity (thought to be important in the jobs) was discouraged by the director's highly authority management and structured styled as well as new director personal work attitude was not good style. It seemed that this new director had unsuitable personal management skill to lead this KBTZ different departments to follow whose guidelines to finish their jobs daily, to cause these departments ' staffs felt dissatisfactory to this new director's personal work attitude . It seemed that this was new director's personal management attitude problem. Moreover, this business office and programming department's survey also indicated these departments existed these problems in KBTZ television station organization.

Firstly, although most of operation department associates were satisfied with their jobs and reported pride in their departments and only some associates felt satisfactory about their operations department manager (head). All other some associates tended to feel overworked (reported a 74 hours workweek) and thought the department head expected too much and who also thought who were underpaid relative to their task demands and criticized managerial feedbacks on their performance and the department head never prised position performance and who only regarded them for poor performance and who also reported concern over the conflict with engineering group , but who believed operations and engineering department conflict, whose departments' leaders (managers) should be resolved. It seemed that this operations departments manager could not manage some departments staffs to work in normal hours to cause them to feel unhappy to work and they also felt underpayment and unreasonable feedback on the performance problem. Anyway, the engineering department many associates were very dissatisfied with whose jobs and who had conflict to operational department and who also believed engineering department head did not support them and who lacked department meetings to receive feedback on their performance from the chief engineer. It seemed that this engineering department's chief engineer who performed more poor to compare to operations department manager to cause

many associates felt dissatisfactory to him. Otherwise, the survey indicated that only promotion department associates had positive attitudes and their

job satisfaction were high and everyone viewed their task environment positively
and who had only few negative attitudes were primarily directed toward the ineffectiveness of the news department . It seemed that promotion department had none any problems, so its
associates could criticize the another news department ineffectiveness result confidently.

Finally, the sales department's colleagues could not responded to the survey to indicate whether what kinds of problems who felt .Due to sale department head was the KBTZ
television station manager's son family relationship , so who could not respond to complete this survey whether whose feelings to this sales department manager was satisfactory or was not satisfactory to him, it would cause who lost their job if who responded whose actual feelings to me (consultant) to know at that day possibly.

Which organization development techniques should I consider using and why?

As I was KBTZ television station consultant, I should apply these organization development techniques to solve this company problems. Organizational development techniques included relationship techniques, such as T-group training,
team building, survey as well as structural technique, such as management by objective and supplemental organizational processes. The news department problem, such as high stress to this department managers and associates. It was respect to time deadlines in television problem. The department's staffs must be on the air with the news. All of the news material , local reporting , news , interviews must be processed, edited and ready to go at six o'clock. So, this news department staffs often worried about extended deadlines or who only half prepared material or who lost the audience, it caused conflict and a
number of well qualified and motivated employees would leave this KBTZ television station organization and KBTZ also felt trouble hiring new qualified people could adapt KBTZ organization's culture to help KBTZ organization to raise competition in this USA entertainment market. On the other hand, due to news department staffs who were confused all of the time, so it also caused operations department manager who felt difficult co-operation with to cause operations department and news department would be often conflicts about news department extended time deadline issue.

Even, program department director also complained the station was missing a lot of opportunities in other areas, e.g. news and sales. I should use organization development technology, relationship technique T-group training to solve

this news and operation departments cooperation problem, which meant news department would implement group exercises in which individual focused on their action, how

others perceived their actions and how others generally reacted to them, so participants often learnt about unintended. Hence, this news department managers and associates who could

divided several groups, it aimed to focus on their individual action, e.g. local reporting group, news report group, interviews group, news material preparing group. So, these every group members (staffs) who could perceived whose individual group action and reacted to another group individual member action, such as news material preparing group individual member could focus on gathering news material preparing job duties, then who could gave news material to news report group individual member to prepare to analyse materials to prepare to report.

Another interviews group individual to prepare how much time needed and what places should be choose and who to be interviewed to prepare every day different news to let

audience to watch six o'clock news programs in television every day. Then, who could gave local reporting group individual member to analyze their every individual interviewing

record to produce every local reporting. Thus, T-group training benefit was that participants, such as KBTZ news department's material group individual member, local reporting group individual member, news production group individual member, interviewed group individual member who could often learnt about why unintended negative consequences were caused of

certain types of any group individual member's behaviour to cause to extend time deadlines or to cause only extend time deadlines or to cause only half prepared material due to very few time was enough to prepare precisely at six o' clock to ready to go before this news department all groups must be

processed to edit. Hence, group member which needed to finish whose identified group job, e.g. interview group members who only needed to focus on carry on training how to make date and time appointment to meet individual in the beginning to till to how to prepare what kinds of interview questions would enquire and every interview was planned which needed how long time to finish. Hence, such as interview group individual member could review whose every interview progress to aim to achieve to shorten time to perform the better news programs quality to provide to television audients to watch at everyday six o'clock news time. Hence, the news department's

every group member could give chance to enquire survey feedback from every team leader (manager)

to review their everyday news job to investigate whether whose group performance would cause unintended negative consequences to influence other group performance to be poor, such as investigating the day's news extended causing was due to the day interview group's individual member who could not organize overall interview procedure to arrange time to finish effectively or other group's individual member to cause. Hence, relationship technique T-group training method could review whether which group(s) to cause the day news extended deadlines or found whether which group(s) caused overall team which could not prepare all material to finish the day news

watching at six o'clock . It was one fair method to measure whether which group staffs were qualified people or whether which group staffs were not qualified people to co-operate in this news department.

Other problem was about business department head, business manager seemed that who lacked management training to prepare to do this position, such as who previously worked to do this position, such as who previously worked in sales and in the general manager's office only. Hence, who must need to provide training to prepare to know how to manage KBTZ 's television station organization different departments, such as news department, sales department, operations department, engineering department, program department, promotion department efficiently. As I was KBTZ 's consultant , I felt KBTZ could provide relationship technique of survey method

to assist whom. If every departments could get survey, then this business manager could obtain enough dates to meet all units to discuss problems easily. Then, when who collected all departments' problems from this survey, KBTZ could use structural technique of management by objectives method to assist him (business manager), it meant a management process in which individuals (different group members) negotiated whose group daily task objectives, such as engineer group

member could negotiate how much equipments who needed to repair urgently and how many equipments who could repair and gave reasons why who could not repair some equipments in

that day. All departments might have task objectives to measure whose every group members performance to revise what factors caused whose performance to be poor in order to correct

to achieve every department's group member could raise work efficiently. Thus, this management process needed spend much time to revise every department's group individual negotiate task. For example, the business manager needed to meet engineering group leader (chief engineer) and members(engineers and technicians) to discuss whether how many equipments who needed to repair and whether how many equipments who needed to repair and whether how many equipments who felt who had no much time to repair this week, then next week, this business manager would enquire these engineers to revise whether what reasons occurred to cause who could not repair all machines last week. As this engineer department individual member technician who had negotiated task objectives to let whose chief engineer and engineering manager to know whether who felt that who could finish task to repair how many machines every week, then they could meet to attempt to explain what factors caused them could not repair all equipments further week. Hence, this business manager could used the same management by objectives structural technique method, such as every department individual member needed to negotiate task objective to finish every week, then who needed to meet whose department manager to revise what factors influenced their work efficiency, e.g. news department material group could meet to discuss task objective about how much time and how many staffs who needed to prepare to gather any related material to report this week ; interview group could meet to discuss task objective about how much time and

how many staffs who needed to prepare to organize any effective interview procedure to prepare individual interview this week ; news edited group could meet to discuss task objective about how much time and how many staffs who needed to be edit for daily news this week. Thus, this

business manager could know all department's every group individual task objectives per week clearly, then who could meet them to attempt to find whether what factors which caused any department's group individual member who could not achieve whose last week objectives efficiently and effectively.

The new director seemed have unsuitable personal management style to lead whose different departments to work together to cause their dissatisfaction to him in this KBTZ television

station organization. For example, the news department felt this new director lacked leadership ability to led news department managers and associates communicate easily. Moreover, news

department associates also complained of very low reward, including pay, promotion opportunities and managerial praise and who also complained of constant criticism , which was the only form of managerial feedback on performance. Hence, it implied the new director did not attempt to solve any departments staffs difficulties to adopt new organization development change to cause their dissatisfaction and conflicts and complaints occurrence to whom. I should suggest this new director as a leader who needed to find method to help different

department leader(manager) to lead whose associates to feel this KBTZ organization must earn more beyond the past by providing a rationale for change currently and let them to feel

guilt and poor anxiety about this KBTZ organization chose not to change and create a sense of psychological safety to them to concern the change, such as news department associates who

complain of low reward, including low promotion opportunities and managerial praise and who also complained of constant criticism feedback on performance. It seemed that who would also complain about low reward, low promotion opportunities and managerial praise and unfair feedback on performance to this new director , even who had good personal managerial style to lead all departments to work. A reason was why these departments, such as news department colleagues complained as above issues because who felt the new director could not adopt to work due to KBTZ sudden change to cause who should be de-commit and dissatisfactory form the status. Hence, this

new director needed to let who to know KBTZ organization would cause poor anxiety and guilt to them in the future if KBTZ organization did not change at this moment as well as this new director might create of psychological discomfort to these departments to let them to know that organization

would loss from its television competitions, even it would dismiss who if KBTZ television station should not choose to change at this moment, such as the negative outcomes would be made and KBTZ 's managers and associates would suffer if changes were not made. Moreover, this business manager also needed to remind every department members that as well as who also needed to downward members to know this who individual would need to change to adopt this new organization change culture to every department in large meetings. Even, this new director also needed to let every department manager (leader) to know how this change process needed to carry on and every department manager also needed to implement evaluation systems to track every department's group individual expected behaviours and work performance whether whose work were more efficiently or whose work were not more efficiently during this KBTZ organization was carrying

on changing at the same time. Hence, every department manager could create efficient reward systems that reinforce every department's group individual's expected behaviours and who could also ensure that whether the hiring and promotion systems which could support all departments colleagues new demands. Especially, news departments felt low reward dissatisfaction. Hence, it could measure whether who ought to raise reward or who ought not to raise reward of their work performance to evaluate more efficiently and effectively.

In conclusion, this KBTZ organization leader (new director) ought attempt to let all departments staffs to know why it needed to change organization style and what would be the disadvantages to any departments colleagues if it decided not change at this moment. Then, I believed that department staffs complaints would be reduced and who would feel more fair to pay reward after who knew how who needed to do whose task to adopt this employer to feel satisfactory.

3. What could have been done to manage the group process better?

To ensure commitment , satisfaction and strong performance among these five MBA student A-team group, the team leader must carefully build and communicate the case for diversity by citing the forces of change discussed earlier and who must ensure fair decision processes and fair outcomes for these other four members. MBA students need to form a group work on a real time consulting project for an organization. The MBA project consulting team course offers valuable on consultancy experience and will have a positive impact on a student's professional development.

This Big State university arranges these MBA program to middle and higher level managers targets to aim to learn global learning experience . Students need to attend weekend classes on school campus or participate through distance learning technology. This is first year project five student team , this team has a faculty advisor to develop a business plan for start up company, includes developing a marketing plan.

Each team must write a report and a business plan and make an hour long presentation to other students and faculty as well as several executives from multinational companies. Finally, students must earn a passing grade to graduate and every team must finish a business plan and a report to achieve university passing level and who also need to attend meetings to discuss what problems who will encounter when they are carrying on doing this A-team project. This university MBA student A-team project aims to provide these adult MBA students' responsibilities to prepare further work in workplace by training.

I think this university professor Bowell group's advisor has responsibility to give suggestions to this A- team leader to attempt to use these methods to manage the A team group process better in the beginning.

The methods include as below:

. The team leader ought organize times and dates in work schedule/ calendar to ensure commitment to meetings to A- team group to work efficiently and effectively.

. This A-team leader ought give confidential university documents to every members to sign to let them to know what their roles and duties are needed to do this project prior to commencement of placement. So if they felt they were not suitable or had interest to share role to do their duties from this leader arrangement, they can enquire to change their roles and duties, then they can decide to sign this consent documents immediately . It will reduce their complains and conflicts occurrence to cause A-team to be disbanded chance.

. This university professor Bowell group's advisor ought to attempt to help A -team members to select a project leader in the beginning. The university professor Bowell group's advisor ought tell this project leader clear duties, e.g. this A-team project leader will act as a main contact point for queries and follow up with the every A-team members to give them feedbacks, he also needs to maintain confidentiality at all times regarding information learned when they are carrying on working on this project.

.This A-team leader needs own characteristics to deal team members conflict. Such as:

He/She needs to manage different types of conflict and group performance and satisfaction, focusing on the content of interpersonal interactions rather than delivery style, explicitly discussing reasons behind any decisional reached in accepting and distributing work assignments and assigning work to members who have the relevant task expertise rather than assigning by other common means such as volunteering or convenience.

. The A-team is successful over time are likely to be proactive in anticipating the need for conflict resolution and in developing conflict resolution strategies that apply to all group members. Leader is key role for conflict management, a process for managing conflict can help to reduce the negative impact of all types of conflict by restoring fairness, process effectiveness, resource efficiency, working relationships and/or satisfaction of parties. So, this A-team leader needs to understand every team member's ability to successfully learn and adapt task strategies to meet performance criteria. Moreover, he/she needs have an overall conflict management process encompasses a wide range of activities, including communication, problem solving, dealing with emotion and understanding positions in the team.

In conclusion, the most importance, this A team leader needs to give recommendations to solve whose another four members conflict from his/her every member opinions.